Thomas Smith Webb Chapter of Research

Thomas Smith Webb Chapter of Research

Transactions 2014-2015, 2023-2025

Edited by Ken JP Stuczynski

cyphrGlyffe
An imprint of Amorphous Publishing Guild
Buffalo, NY USA

www.Amorphous.Press

Contents

Disclaimer

No individual or institution speaks for all Masons. There is no "official" dogma, as even the Landmarks of the Craft vary in number and interpretation across the jurisdictional landscape. Those who are Companions, having passed the veils and being exalted, should have doubly learned this precept.

Any Masonic writing should be taken as the views, opinions, and beliefs of its respective author. They are not to prove or persuade, but give consideration to facts and ideas. Exposure to individual differences broadens our own understanding, and even if we disagree on some point, at least we know another view exists. We may then accept it as part of our collective body of what is held to be true.

Contradictions are not failures, but a transcendence of the limitations of a solitary mind. Be it your truth, my truth, or our truth, it is the exercise and journey of these disciplines that ultimately bring us closer to Truth, or at least, to face the East and move a step closer to that which we seek. In the end, each of us maintains the right to accept or reject these as building blocks for our own intellectual edifice; it is ultimately our own responsibility to discern where a truth is to be found, and how we find it to be so.

– *The Editor*

From the Grand High Priest

I want to congratulate the Thomas Smith Webb Chapter of research for continuing to set the example for the rest of the world. We provide an atmosphere where people can feel that their creative ideas are appreciated and encouraged. I am a proud member of the chapter and want to thank all of the members who contributed informative papers to be published in this book. A huge thank you needs to go to E.·. Ken Stuczynski, the current High Priest of Thomas Smith Webb, for putting all of this together for publication. Our attendance has grown exponentially over the last few years under the direction of M.·.E.·. Williamson, M.·.E.·. Huck,

R.·.E.·. Gregg, and E.·. Stuczynski, and I look forward to enjoying the excitement that is growing from all of our new members. I hope Companions take the time to read all of the papers included and are motivated to not only participate in the research chapter but also to write a paper of their own for presentation. Our hope is to continue to invite like-minded individuals into this great chapter.

Let's learn from the past and build for the future!

In Fervency and Zeal,

M.·.E.·. Mark G. Peerson
Grand High Priest 2025-2026

Editor's Note

The Thomas Smith Webb Chapter of Research began in 2002, but the first two publications of Transactions covered the years 2010 and 2011. These volumes, "Transactions 2010" and "Transactions 2011", were edited by William Thomas (Grand Master of Masons in the State of New York, 2014-2016) and were published on Lulu as eBooks. They are currently available for $9.99 each.

The 2010 volume contains the following papers:

- *Symbolism & Freemasonry as a Mystery School* by Piers Vaughan
- *Jonathan Harrington* – Patriot and Mason by Ronald M. Goldwyn
- *Scottish Royal Arch Masonry* by Grant Macleod
- *The Mark Degree in Scotland* by Grant Macleod
- *The Excellent Master Degree in Scotland* by Grant Macleod

The 2011 volume contains the following papers:

- *Circumambulation* by Piers Vaughan

- *Dansville Bible* by Bill Thomas
- *The Labyrinth* by Walter Slodki
- *RAM Centennial Commemorative Coin, 1898* by Bill Thomas
- *Cedars Chapter, Beirut, Lebanon* by Razmig Djinbachian
- *Royal Arch & Irish Freemasonry* by James Penny
- *The Arch …* by George Lloyd Simpson
- *The Hero's Journey* by Tony Denny
- *Truth, Which Is Zerubbabel* by Jeffrey G. Burcham

This current volume is a compilation of all the available presentations given by Companions of the Thomas Smith Webb Chapter of Research that were available and not previously published. The first section is from papers presented in the years immediately following the publication of the first two volumes, those available having been presented in 2014 and 2015.

The Chapter did not meet for a number of years until 2023, an initiative of Past Grand High Priest Jeffrey Williamson. (I was elected as Scribe, and now serve as Excellent High Priest as of the writing of this work.) The second section comprises papers presented from that time to the present. There were other presentaions that were not in written form, or not made available by the presenter. These may be included in future editions.

The general style guide is that of The Quarry Project with a few modifications, but the content of the papers themselves may honor the conventions of their respective authors. Edits and corrections were kept to a minimum, and no substantive changes were made. Earlier papers (2014-2015) are ordered alphabetically by the author's surname; the order of papers since 2023 is chronological, based on when they were presented (or sent to the membership if not presented).

This volume will be available worldwide in softcover and eBook (including access through library apps). Though some of the content is esoteric, it is unlikely any "secrets" of the Craft will become legible or intelligible from these works.

It is my hope at some future time to develop a composite tome of all three volumes plus additional works, similar to the hardcover "Books of Transactions 1983-2013" I edited and published for the Western New York Lodge of Research. In the meantime, I hope the reader finds this third volume of our Research Chapter enlightening as both a preservation of our work and a tangible testament to our fervency and zeal.

E/Comp. Ken JP Stuczynski
High Priest, Thomas Smith Webb Chapter of Research
Editor, "Transactions 2014-2025"
18 February 2026

Preface

Masonic Research Societies in general, and Capitular Research Societies in particular, are essential for growth and fulfillment in the quest for further light within our great fraternity. There is nothing more rewarding than digging deep into research and discovering that wonderful, long-forgotten "vein of gold"— busting off the mud and hauling it up, bringing it to the surface, so that all may enjoy "that which was lost." Through this process, we learn and appreciate the history and philosophy of our heritage.

The Thomas Smith Webb Research Chapter was formally warranted by the Grand Chapter State of New York on August 2, 2002, marking a significant milestone in our commitment to Masonic scholarship and research.

I am deeply grateful to Most Excellent Jason Sheridan GHP 2022 for charging me to reignite the fire and passion of the Chapter, and for welcoming all those new Companions who joined us to get back on track. I know that our founding fathers – RE Stephen A. Rubinstein, RE John Mark Hilliard, and especially ME Ted Harrison – would be pleased to see our renewed progress.

My sincerest gratitude goes to E/ Kenneth Stuczynski for gathering these papers, and to RE Oscar Alleyne for preserving and bringing forward papers to be included in this book.

I extend my best wishes for our future prosperity and growth. May our existing Officers continue to nurture this fine organization for many years to come!

With fraternal regards,

Jeffrey M. Williamson
GHP 2010, and Fellow

PART I

Transactions 2014-2015

{The content in this section was originally to be compiled as the "Thomas Smith Webb Chapter of Research Transactions 2014-2015" but was never published until now.}

1

What is the Relationship between Companionship and Freemasonry?

OSCAR ALLEYNE

JEAN-MICHEL MATHONIÈRE, DIRECTOR OF THE CENTRE FOR THE STUDY OF GUILDS (AVIGNON) OVERVIEW AND ENGLISH TRANSLATION BY OSCAR ALLEYNE

{Dr. E. Oscar Alleyne, Junior Grand Warden of the Grand Lodge of New York from 2018-2021, is a member of several Lodges and bodies of Research, including Quatuor Coronati No.2076, and is a past President and Fellow of both the Masonic Society and Philalethes Society.}

Overview

Compagnonnage refers to an organization of French craftsmen and artisans usually made up of men involved in similar trades.

A *Compagnon* means "companion, craftsman or journeyman". Translated from Old French and Latin, the word literally means: "He with whom one shares one's bread."

The earliest traces of Compagnonnage date back to the Middle Ages, when the first Companionship associations made their appearance in the 16th century. Most of the earliest records of these Companions are found in judicial archives due to many disputes between them at that time. It is through these documents that there was proof of the existence of groups of young journeymen who traveled, helped one another, practiced rituals in various circumstances, and possessed common attributes and vocabulary. For example, from 1514 up until the 1580s, Companion Printers in Lyons and Geneva were organized into protective associations, traveled, went on strike, carried out reception ceremonies and used secret handshakes and other signs of recognition.

From the 16th to the mid-19th century, Companion guilds flourished. By the end of the 19th century, there existed some thirty guilds and approximately as many trades known as Devoirs ("Duties"). Each of which was organized with its own rules, its own particular customs, specific vocabulary, rites and symbols, secret words, attributes, etc. Even though the different guilds had many commonalities, each had a strong sense of its own identity. Their traditional, technical education training includes taking a tour around France and being the apprentice of competent masters.

For a young man, the Compagnonnage represented an original way to learn a trade, while developing character by experiencing community life and traveling. The community would live in a Companion house, which could have 5 people to more than 100 people living together. It is estimated that there were more than 80 Companion houses in France by the end of the 19th Century. Until recently, the Companion members were all male. Today, Compagnons can be found in 49 countries practicing many different trades.

While many of us are familiar with the international cycling competition called the Tour de France, the Compagnonnage also have a Tour de France which describes the requirement for members to work in different places in France, changing work locations every six months to a year. To start a *Tour de France*, the initiate is required to already have a *Certificat d'Aptitude Professionelle* diploma which includes classes and an apprenticeship. This and the following described stages are essential in order to become a member.

Stagiaire: During the first year of the *Tour de France*, the initiate's title is a *Stagiaire (Compagnon Guest)*. Full-time work in a trade begins and there is a requirement to live in the Companion house. Lessons on their trade are set at specific times during the week and dinner is eaten communally at the *siège* (lodge) of Compagnons. During this period, if the Companion life is agreeable and, the initiate can apply for the adoption ceremony to be part of the family

Ceremony of Adoption: In this stage a *Travail d'adoption* is required, which is a project that must be submitted to become an Aspirant. At this point, the initiate may be adopted as an Aspirant and receives a fraternal name, which is derived from the region or town that the initiate comes from in France. For example, somebody from Burgundy, will be called Bourguignon. The Aspirant is also presented with a sash and a ceremonial walking staff. This walking staff is a distinctive feature of the Compagnons, representing the itinerant nature of the organization.

Aspirant: Aspirants begin working full-time in their trade while continuing to live in the Companion house. Lessons are again set at specific times during the week and dinner is eaten communally at the siège (lodge) of Compagnons. Aspirants stay in several towns over the next three to five years, working under Compagnons to further learn their trade.

Ceremony of Reception: Before a *Reception* ceremony can be held, *Aspirants* must present their masterpiece (*travail de réception*) to the board of Compagnons. The masterpiece is a required piece, which every kind of Companion must complete as an Aspirant to become a Companion. Of course, there are different kinds of masterpieces depending on the trade. If accepted, he may become a *Compagnon Itinérant* and receive an official Companion name. Furthermore, he is presented with a new walking stick that reaches "the height of his heart".

Compagnon: During the three years following the *Reception*, the initiate is called *Compagnon itinérant* because of the requirement to do three more years of touring. Thereafter, the initiate is a *Compagnon Sedantaire*. There is no longer a requirement to tour, as the Companion can live and work anywhere he or she wishes. The Companion can also volunteer to teach the younger members various methods of the trade. One area of interest are the allegorical lessons taught to initiates in their progression to becoming Companions.

Companion Legends

The Companionship uses an Old Testament Biblical narrative in their esoteric teachings, referring to Kings V of the Bible which speaks about the building of the temple, King Solomon and describes three kinds of workers: carriers, builders and leaders. The Companion legend uses three mythological figures: King Solomon, who was told by his father (King David) to build the first temple of the Jews; Master Jacques who was the architect of the temple; and Father Soubise who was the second architect and a friend of Master Jacques.

A main character named Hiram was said to be the builder of Solomon's temple. He was also the master and initiator of certain mysteries. A story states that hidden under Solomon's temple was a secret temple for the initiated which was in use while the building was still in process. Hiram travaillait le bronze et il était rempli de sagesse, d'intelligence et de science. Hiram is said to have been skilled in working bronze and was filled with wisdom, understanding and knowledge. Pour payer les ouvriers, en éliminant les intrus et les oisifs qui se mêlaient à eux, Hiram donna à chacun des ouvriers un nouveau mot de passe pour se faire reconnaître. Hiram gave each worker a new password to be recognized in order to pay workers and eliminate intruders and idlers who mingled with them. Ainsi, chacun était payé selon son mérite et recevait, le moment venu, les assignations et les mots de passe qui lui permettaient de se faire reconnaître. Therefore everyone was paid according to his merit, and received, in due course, assignments and passwords that allowed him to be recognized.

It is said that Holem, Sterkin and Hoterfut were three apprentices regarded as being unfit for initiation into these mysteries. They conspired to obtain the password from Hiram and killed him in their attempt. Later when they came back at night to dispose of his body, they dug three holes, one for his clothes, one for his cane and the other for his corpse. Solomon sent nine Companions in search of the missing Hiram. They found the burial sites by the presence of a branch of acacia. Solomon ordered all the Companions to shave their beards, cut their hair and wear a white apron in mourning. ils portèrent aussi des gants blancs indiquant qu'ils étaient innocents du meurtre. They also wore white gloves indicating that they were innocent of the murder. Solomon then changed the password for certainty and the three were punished.

In another legend, Jacques and Soubise are friends who worked together as architects on the temple. They however got into arguments and had a physical fight. Their followers got very hostile towards each other's camp and followers of Soubise are said to have killed Jacques.

Another legend is often used to explain the origin of the three orders of Compagnons. Around 1267 to 1369, a split occurred with the architects responsible for building the great towers of the Cathedral of Orleans. There were two architects at work named Jacques de Moler and Antoine Soubise. The Companion Order referred to as "children of Salomon" claim to descend from Salomon and are the original order where as the orders that referred to as the "children of Master Jacques" and "the children of Father Soubise" resulted after the schism.

"The children of Salomon" are considered to have been the builders of the temple that replaced the tabernacle for the Jews. In later days they became the builders of the gothic cathedrals. "The children of Master Jacques" are also known as the "Compagnons Passant" and "Companions de Devoir" who were later mostly concerned with the building of bridges. The third are "the children of Father Soubise" were later responsible for the construction of ecclesiastical buildings in the Romanesque style.

Companionship and Freemasonry

One of the questions most frequently asked about the French system of Companionship is if there is a relationship with Freemasonry. To the uninitiated, the use of an identical emblem of **the interlaced square and compasses** reinforces that idea. In addition, the mysterious side and elitism of the two organizations induces some to believe that they are somehow two faces of the same secret society. Some have a firm belief of a close relationship considering Freemasons as the first cousins of the Companions. Others even consider the possibility that Freemasonry borrowed most of its craft degrees from Companionship.

The fact remains that for some time, historians of both organizations have been tackling these theories in spirited debates without managing to arrive at a consensus. Freemasons, fascinated by the descendants of the medieval builders of cathedrals, feel that the legacy of the French Companions should be clear and evident. This however remains to be seen historically, in terms of initiation and affiliations. Without going back to those ancient times where some records and archives are cruelly lacking, what is exactly

Compagnon Cordonnier-Bottier du Devoir.

the link between Companionship and Freemasonry? Let us focus on some aspects of this complex issue.

Dual membership

As history informs, Masonry and Companionship did not seem to visibly interact. Many a Companion cultivated anti-Masonic or less than positive attitude towards Freemasonry. This was inherited from the Vichy period when France was occupied in World War 1 and a wartime government based in the city of Vichy, south of Paris from July 1940 to 1944 before Allied liberation. It was during this period that the French had a deep Companionship upheaval and divisions. Thus, in a large number of Companionships, dual affiliation was strictly prohibited and any discovery of a violation of this rule, lead to removal of the member from the organization. In other Companionships, an individual had a certain freedom of choice which served to warn the Companion wanting to become a Freemason of the difficulty that may be encountered in meeting all his obligations as a Companion and as a Mason. Historical evidence supported the assertion that some dual membership existed. There was a tradition within certain circles of the Union Companionship where a number of its founders in 1889 were Masons. Though rare, there were examples within the Federation Companionship (the construction trades), including among the Gavots (Companions carpenters and locksmiths, and the Duty of Freedom, which was affiliated with the famous Agricola Perdiguier himself who joined Freemasonry in 1845).

Compagnon Cloutier du Devoir.
(ancienne tenue d'enterrement)

There were significant variations to the dual membership phenomenon, which mostly depended on the business and Companionship rites, and also according to the time period. For example, throughout the nineteenth century, membership in Freemasonry was very common, if not almost systematically, among the Companion Foreign Fellow Stone Cutters (the branch that claims lineage to Solomon). Dual membership was relatively widespread among the Companion Passers Stone Cutters (the other branch, claiming lineage as the "children" of Master Jacques) before the Revolution of 1789 but becomes very rare afterwards. The same was seen among the Companion Carpenters, where dual membership is commonplace in some groups while virtually being unknown in "Soubise".

What were the reasons for these dual memberships in the past? Is the answer the implicit recognition of a relationship between Companionship and Freemasonry? Not necessarily. Two main causes seem to emerge from the study of documented sources.

Firstly, it is well known from the mid-19th Century that there was the desire for some Companions to foster fraternal friendliness with Masons largely based on shared symbolism. This was generally seen among Companions who completed their Tour de France now having more contacts with Freemasons within their social circles. The second claim arose from the need for traveling itinerant workers to network with others, including Freemasons, in order to cope with the vagaries of the Tour de France.

A number of Companions of the early 19th Century joined Freemasonry during the Tour de France route, to benefit from networks of mutual assistance. In cities that did not have Companionship organizations, they would still be able to rely upon the Masonic fraternity to provide support and relief. In addition to these two reasons, a number of Companions who served in the army during that period, were able to join Freemasonry via the various military lodges that existed.

True Similarities?

The use of the recognizable emblem of the interlaced square and compasses in Companionship was indisputably used by some guilds before the arrival of Freemasonry in France. It is important not to see this as an indication of the influence of one on the other, and even less evidence of a Companionship origin to Freemasonry.

In fact, the Companions, like the Freemasons, use the square and compasses to refer to the fifth Liberal Art of Geometry, which is fundamental for both groups. Why? If one considers this common symbol as the index of an organic relationship, then it is just one of the signs of the existence of a common cultural substrate of Architecture. These same geometrical instruments were publicly used at that time as symbols of the arts and sciences, or as moral emblems, without necessarily being associated as the emblem belonging to any one organization. For example, the compass is, as the serpent, an emblem of Prudence or Caution.

An area of interest for Masons are the few published excerpts of Companionship rituals including the 1901 classic work of Stephen Martin St. Leon: *The Companionship*. Whole sections of ritual can be compared and matched with Freemasonic ritual of the "Rite Français" (French Rite), which was used in the late 19th century by the Grand Orient of France. Is this not, as believed by Jean-Pierre Bayard, clear evidence of an undeniable link between the two orders? No, it is simply one of the many ceremonial, legendary or iconographic loans made by operative guilds to Masonic sources throughout the 19th Century. This is because there were Companions who "dove" into Masonic traditions, but not the reverse.

Why was that? Are these loans the result of the phenomenon of dual membership previously mentioned? In doing so, would the Companions not recognize a priority of the Masonic tradition to their own? No and no. There was no need for Companions that "double-dipped" to betray their Masonic oath at the end of 18th

Century, as it was possible for anyone who could read to get most Masonic rituals in libraries and bookstores. A number of Companions knew how to read, as seen in library copies of classics, such as works of Guillemain Saint-Victor's coated bookplate *Compagnonniques*. In 1843, Clavel's the "Illustrated History of Freemasonry and Ancient and Modern Secret Societies" was a favorite book, as evidenced by the beautiful engravings and illustrations found in the book being used and borrowed for Companionship prints of that time (See Laurent Bastard *Images of the Companions of the Tour de France*).

So what was the reason for the borrowing of these images? The ancient rituals and legends of Companionship were relatively sober and Christian in essence. In the "Resolution of Doctors of the Sorbonne" in 1655, which pointed concerns on the "ungodly, sacrilegious and superstitious practices" of Companion saddlers, shoemakers, cutlers, hatters and tailors, are for the most part describing the staging of the Passion, where the winner will be deemed as Christ by suffering and dying before being reborn.L'arrivée de la franc-maçonnerie spéculative et l'évolution des mentalités sous la Révolution va chambouler cette trame rituelle restée stable jusque vers la fin du XVIII e siècle. The arrival of speculative Freemasonry and the changing attitudes during the Revolution shook up the Companionship ritual frame that remained stable until the late 18th Century.

Quite naturally, the Companions sought to give their rites and legends the fashion and mentality of their time, enriched in great detail and adventures. In the late 1860's, Jules Napoleon Bastard (a Companion Tanner), who will become a Freemason some years later, wrote the following lines relating to the reforms to be introduced in his Companionship society. He notably amplifies the reception to give a more emotional charge, which may summarize the fascination Companions had with Freemasonry:

> "But what do we have to be able to teach a man? Nothing, our writings are not quite complicated enough, it lacks great things [...] What will it take? A well written book containing the details from which Companionship companies stem, the rank of each body of the state, boost our reception, increase our recognition [...] Let us walk in the footsteps of Masons without mimicking their principles, as there is nothing to borrow from them... for our receptions, witnessing it with a suitable setting, that is to say, in a frock coat, tall hat, fitted our colors with a decent upgrade, i.e. in frock coats, tall hat, fitted with our colors. Also have the blue apron embroidered in white and red, our tools will be above, the two columns of the temple and the compasses & square [...] a transparent representation of the two pillars of the temple, the olive branch, a compass & a square [...] the dog of Perignan, a tomb behind the veil, all the companions sitting and the first in the city will interview the recipient, will introduce with a spin, blindfolded in chamber, only the will left to write on these reflections, having before him a coffin covered with a pall and two white colors representing the cross, two rods above the coffin, a pistol; a dagger, the sun and the moon painted on glass in the form of a lantern. That is the country that we need."

It must be highlighted that, despite the language used to suggest otherwise, the details given about wearing an apron and the decoration of the temple are purely borrowing from Freemasonry.

Compagnon Couvreur du Devoir.
(mêmes insignes pour le Plâtrier)

A common cultural substrate

In fact, the first error to be made when discussing the delicate issue of a relationship between Freemasonry and Companionship is to consider it as being homogeneous. This is not the case at all, especially if one goes back centuries. It is more appropriate to speak of guilds in plural.

In fact, if any form of relationship must be sought, it is not between the Freemasonic tradition and all of the Companionship guilds indiscriminately, but first with the guilds of stone-masons. It is not between speculative Freemasonry, as it gets Europeanized by the middle of the 18th century, and the French guilds of stone-masons (the *passers* and *foreigners*), but between the Scottish and English operative lodges.

And the problem is not to become obsessed over the ritual kinship, but to better identify and understand the common cultural substrate of all these organizations. This can be seen in the trades and the arts and related sciences whether or not they have an initiatory characteristic. Such serious and methodical exploration certainly promises a pathway for great discoveries.

REFERENCES

Jean-Michel Mathonière. Director of the Centre for the Study of Guilds (Avignon) Webmaster www.compagnons.info

- "The Secret Plan Hiram speculative operative foundations and prospects Table Lodge", ed. Dervy, 2012.
- "The Rule and Compass", the eponymous exhibition catalog, ed. Museum of Freemasonry Masonry, 2013.
- "The Serpent compassionate, iconography and symbolism of the crest of the Companions stonemasons", ed. The Ship of Solomon, 2010.

Museum of Compagnonnage. http://www.museecompagnonnage.fr/compagnonnage-histoire-an.html

Michele Montemurro. The Operating Tradition of the Compagnonnage du Devoir du Tour de France

2

A Deeper Inspection of the Virtual Past Master Degree

WILLIAM CARTER

BROTHERS! Now, we shall make an advance in mind and heart, as we explore the Virtual Past Master Degree. Originally, when Chapters of Royal Arch Masonry were under the government of Lodges in which it was a regulation that no one could receive the Royal Arch Degree unless he had previously presided in the Lodge as Master. When the Chapters became independent, the regulation could not be abolished, because that would have been an innovation. Therefore, the Virtual Past Master Degree was instituted to make it possible for all worthy Mark Master Masons to receive the Royal Arch Degree. The first record of its conferral is found in 1768 in England.

While this degree is much less spoken of in regard to its deep mystical impression than that of the more notable Holy Royal

Arch, The Virtual Past Master Degree is no less important and rich with esoteric symbolism that deserves our contemplation. Now, it's true that it is not an elaborate degree. Its ceremonies are simple. But the requirement for a brother to receive the Past Master's Degree before moving on to the Most Sublime Degree of the Holy Royal Arch is of great significance. It is a reminder that one should be a Past Master of the labors of the craft if he is to progress in Freemasonry. It is of the utmost importance to study, practice, and master the lessons of the Blue Lodge Degrees in order to be mentally and spiritually mature enough to advance along the mystic paths within the York Rite.

First, let's define what a master is.

According to Merriam-Webster's Dictionary, a master is:

1. a :(1) : a male teacher (2) : a person holding an academic degree higher than a bachelor's but lower than a doctor's
   b: often capitalized: a revered religious leader
   c : a worker or artisan qualified to teach apprentices
   d : (1) : an artist, performer, or player of consummate skill (2) : a great figure of the past (as in science or art) whose work serves as a model or ideal

2. a : one having authority over another: ruler, governor
   b : one that conquers or masters: victor, superior <in the new challenger the champion found his master>
   c : a person licensed to command a merchant ship
   d :(1) : one having control (2) : an owner, especially of a slave or animal
   e : the employer, especially of a servant
   f :(1) dial husband (2): the male head of a household

The implication is that a master is one who, through dedication and countless hours of study, practice, instruction, and labor, has achieved the pinnacle of the required skills, and is now able to demonstrate that skill in his work and transmit that skill to his apprentices as the master craftsman of the operative stonemason guilds had done from time immemorial.

A master craftsman or master tradesman (sometimes called only master or grandmaster, German: Meister) was a member of a guild. In the European guild system, only masters and journeymen were allowed to be members of the guild.

An aspiring master would have to pass through the career chain from apprentice to journeyman before he could be elected to become a master craftsman. He would then have to produce a sum of money and a masterpiece before he could actually join the guild. If the overseers of the guild did not accept the masterpiece he presented, he was not allowed to join, possibly remaining a journeyman for the rest of his life. Originally, holders of the academic degree of "Master of Arts" were also considered, in the medieval universities, as master craftsmen in their own academic field.

Conversely, the speculative master has memorized and internalized the duties of the craft to such a degree that he exemplifies the highest ideals of such as his masterpiece, and earns the highest of spiritual wages for his labor. As such the Master's work becomes the living example of perfection. As the process described is clearly an external endeavor, in speculative masonry, we have used this path to mastery to describe the internal work and craftsmanship of perfecting the self and reaching a state of harmony with the "I AM" Presence. The great work being the subduing of the discordant passions and desires, waging war with the lower self and the illusion of separation until one has usurped the Ego's control over the self, and the higher spiritual presence within claims the seat of authority, and has sovereignty over his carnal nature.

As we alluded to in the Mark Master Degree, one has perfected the labors of his trade and reached a state of proficiency in the duties of apprentice and fellowcraft and is exalted for his achievement to the level of master. As master, he is entitled to the gavel of authority and now is qualified and prepared to open and govern the lodge. The "labor" to which one is now called as a Past Master is he himself. The idea behind the Past Master receiving the gavel is not that he wields authority over the Lodge, but that he has achieved authority over self. An authority that renders him eligible to advance to the most sublime degree of the Holy Royal Arch and beyond in Divine Knowledge to the ends of infinity.

To be a Past Master of the Art is a worthy distinction, but one is not a Past Master in fact unless he endeavors to measure up to the responsibilities implied by the title; a Master of self, a Master of his own passions and prejudices, a Master in leadership of those less informed, submissive only to the Will of God and the laws of a just society, and therefore a Master of his own destiny. To be a Past Master in title alone is meaningless. One must strive to actualize the Past Master within, for he who would assume to govern others must first learn to govern himself.

From the Blue Lodge Degrees to the Holy Royal Arch, the Past Master Degree is the 5th degree. The number 5 is a very dynamic number in all mystery schools of antiquity. In Christianity, it symbolizes God's grace, goodness, and favor toward humans and is mentioned 318 times in Scripture. Multiplied by itself, which is 25, it becomes 'grace upon grace' (John 1:16). The Ten Commandments contain two sets of five commandments. The first five commandments are related to our treatment and relationship with God, and the last five concern our relationship with humanity.

In mysticism, the number five indicates the mastery or command of the active principle or eternal chaos ever present around the finite form. Five symbolizes human suffering and transformation, the turning point in human destiny. Five represents the primordial spirit, fundamental to all beings, that is crucified on the cross of matter, containing the four elements of air, fire, water, and earth. Remember in the Mark Master Degree, the wages (of consequence) have changed from corn, wine, and oil (material form) to coin or gold (spiritual being), representing the perfection of matter. Now, as a past master, your duty refines from just exemplifying the results of the inner work to a state of being the living example of the inner work. Despite our connection to the senses, man must employ free will in order to bolster self-discipline, redirect energies toward the divine, and work toward perfect consciousness. The 5th degree is symbolic of the number of the will, our instrument of reintegration. Initiates recognize that the substitution of five for four is only transitorily disastrous and that the fallen human, by wallowing in the mire of matter, learns how to attain a truly free personality and become more fully aware of higher planes. Consider the allegory of the keystone in the Mark Master Degree, the realization of the true value of the stone to complete the temple. Having then to retrieve the stone from the rubble of the carnal self. Therefore, he rises from his fall, again and again, stronger and greater, because evil only replaces good temporarily, and with the explicit purpose of mental and spiritual evolution.

The Virtual Past Master degree is basically a mock degree of being exalted to the east to rule and govern. So in this degree as opposed to the blue degrees, a candidate is not "initiated" a Past Master. As he has surpassed the sublime degree f Master Mason, he is no longer an initiate. He is said to be "inducted into the Oriental chair." He isn't duly elected to receive the degrees but in a symbolic sense has been bestowed "that distinguished honor." His obligation mirrors that of the Worshipful Master in the east, where one agrees to conduct himself according to the duties of the office. While the obligation holds allegorical value, it is in the grip where the mystic meaning begins to take shape. The newly made Past Master is told, "A two-fold cord is strong, but a three-fold cord is not easily broken." This statement brings the Past Master to remembrance of the completion of the Mark Master Degree, where he contemplates the three dimensions of man demonstrated by completing the 3 craft Degrees of Blue Lodge. Man is body, mind, and spirit, which he, as an Entered Apprentice, Fellowcraft, and Master Mason, has become intimately concerned with. As the Mark Master, one has come to the realization of the equal importance of all three dimensions to the perfection of man. As Past Master, we have been fulfilled and realize that while cooperation of body and mind may make a good man, it is only in union with the spirit that man may realize perfection, and proceed beyond to pursue a deific life. Also alluding to The Messiah Jesus' fulfillment of God's promise to mankind as Father (Spirit/Will), Son (body/manifest), and Holy Ghost (mind/soul or "breath") reunite as one being, and then becomes one with the "I AM".

The Great Light describes man as being in a primordial state in the presence of his Creator. Before the fall, in the Garden of Eden or the etheric plane, man was perfect. Eve, or the feminine passive nature dormant in perfect man, was tempted by the serpent (kundalini, or primordial force) to eat from the apple of the tree of the knowledge of good and evil (duality). (Refer to the wages of a mason.) She, in turn, tempted Adam, the masculine active nature, to do the same. Once eaten, they became "aware of their nakedness" and were ultimately cast out of the garden to "toil the soil". Remember the first question the Entered Apprentice is asked in his proficiency examination? "Whence came you?" The word "Lodge" refers to a state of being rather than a place. "John" comes from the Hebrew "Jochonan," which means, "favored of God." "Jerusalem" means either "the foundation of (the god) Shalem," the patron-god of the city, or "the city of Shalem," which also can be translated as Peace. Thus we came from "A lodge of the Holy Saints' John of Jerusalem", meaning a state of perfect being, completeness, favored of God as the Source.

The second question, "What came you here to do?" alludes to why Adam and Eve (man in duality) were cast out to the soil, or the material plane. Remember the keystone in the Mark Master Degree? How it was not a typical stone, yet beautiful and intriguing, but when presented to the authorities, they didn't recognize its true value, had it thrown into the rubble (or dirt), only to realize it's great purpose at the near completion of the temple? So it is dug out and retrieved from the rubble and exalted to its proper place as the capstone of the arch, finishing the building of the temple? Well, this story is symbolic of the Past Master's spiritual journey through his cycle age! As Adam and Eve, being the perfect man in potential, were cast out and thrown in to the rubble of the material plane, where they toiled the land of the flesh in the labor of spiritual evolution, only to finish the task and reach the station of master of the self, and labor towards the degree of Mark Master, the state of harmony of mind, body, and spirit. Then, as Past Master, he may step aside from the East reborn, and endeavor towards union with the Source. His trestle board is now left as a blueprint for the successors for ages to come.

The Virtual Past Master is symbolically invested with the past master's jewel. The jewel consists of the Compasses placed upon a Quadrant, with the Blazing Sun in the center. The Compasses, extended to Thirty Degrees on each side, totaling to Sixty Degrees, are placed on the Quadrant. Thirty Degrees is the symbol of Rebirth, while Sixty Degrees refers to perfect balance. The space between the Compasses and the Quadrant forms an equilateral triangle. Thus symbolizing the perfect balance between the Perfect Creator and the perfected man. It also shows that the wearer of this jewel has served equally in the South, the West, and the East, symbolizing the three phases of matter being solid, liquid, and gas. The jewel itself can also be seen as a symbol of a sextant. A sextant is a tool of navigation, used to measure altitude and enable one to determine one's location, and thus plot a course to travel. This is an ideal symbol for a Past Master, as he has had to navigate the course of his lodge during his term in the East. Spiritually, he navigates the course of his development, reaching that state of union with the "I AM" Presence that permeates the existence of all. It also shows that he is capable of assisting in the navigation of the Lodge, if his successor needs his assistance. In this role, he provides "wise counsel", as the Great Architect has given him counsel in the mysteries of the craft. The Blazing Sun is placed in the Triangle symbolizing the ever-present Deity, or glory above in the center, enlightening the earth, giving light and life to all things here below. Similarly, the Past Master, while in his tenure, should be a beacon of light, wisdom, and guidance to the members of the lodge. Inwardly, it is the light of truth that now permeates his existence, as the Divine Will is the foundation of his spiritual edifice. He, the Past Master, is inferred to possess the combined Physical and spiritual, which connects Masonry to Universal Law.

In conclusion, while it is human nature to sometimes overlook and pass over ideas we may deem as trivial, this Degree and the symbolism described above are proof that within the tenets of Freemasonry, there is little present that can be viewed as invaluable. It is then within the best interest of every brother who chose to walk within the walls of this sacred temple of wisdom, take heed and note of every sign, symbol, allegory, and ritual available, for hidden deep within the soil of the outward expressions are precious jewels of Divine Truths waiting to be discovered. A true master is not just an adherent of a part of the craft. Rather, he is the living example of the whole of the craft!

3

Exactly Who was Thomas Smith Webb?

MARK D. ISAACS

{Rev. Dr. Mark D. Isaacs was Grand Chaplain at the time of this presentation.}

"Where Webb found disorder and confusion, he arranged and reduced the system, placing everything in its proper relative position, and restoring to the entire ritual order and harmony." —Brother Cornelius Moore (1806-1883)

ONE, TWO, THREE, and FOUR… This is the key to understanding the complex life and work of Thomas Smith Webb.

ONE: Thomas Smith Webb was born on October 30, 1771, and he died in July 6, 1819 in Cleveland, Ohio. He lived most of his life in New England and Upstate New York State during the formative years of the Federalist and Early Republican Period in American history. Major events that occurred during Webb's lifetime include: *The American Revolution* (1774-1783); *The Articles of Confederation* (1781-1787); *Shays' Rebellion* in Western Massachusetts (1786); *The U.S. Constitution* and *The Bill of Rights* (1787-1788); George Washington inaugurated as our first president (1789-1796); the bitter *Election of 1800* [Thomas Jefferson (Democrat-Republican) defeated John Adams (Federalist)]; Mr. Madison's War, i.e., "*The War of 1812* (1812-1815);" and the devastating economic *Panic of 1819*. Internationally, Europe exploded with the bloody and violent *French Revolution* (1789-1799) and then the catastrophic *Napoleonic Wars* (1799-1815).

TWO: Thomas Smith Webb is remembered for *two* major contributions to Freemasonry.

First, on September 14, 1797, he published his landmark book,

Freemason's Monitor or Illustrations of Masonry. The importance of this book cannot be overemphasized. This popular book had a profound impact on "the development of Masonic ritual in America, and especially that of the York Rite."

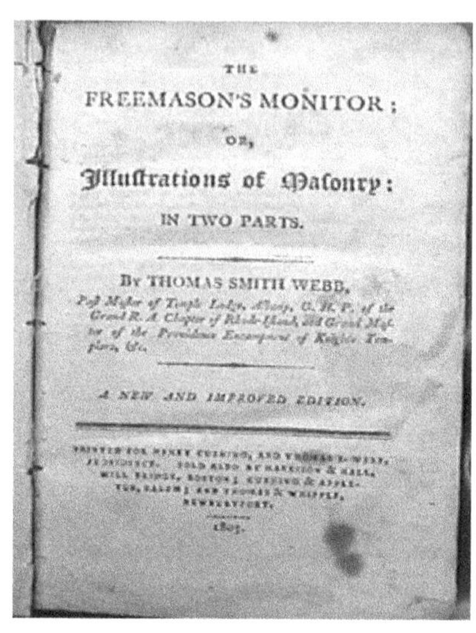

THE

FREEMASON'S MONITOR;

OR,

Illustrations of Masonry:

IN TWO PARTS.

BY THOMAS SMITH WEBB,

A NEW AND IMPROVED EDITION.

Essentially an abbreviation of William Preston's (1742-1818) *Illustrations of Masonry* (1772), Webb edited, rewrote, and re-systematized the entire Blue Lodge Ritual. According to Brother Cornelius Moore (1806-1883), "He had carefully studied the rituals of the old Prestonian Lectures, and he saw the necessity of rearranging them, and reducing them to system and order." In his *Monitor*, Webb also added new material to Preston's work. According to Arturo de Hoyos, 33°, Grand Archivist and Grand Historian of the Supreme Council of the Scottish Rite, Southern Jurisdiction, Webb also "combined Preston's ritual with [material taken from] the [Masonic] exposure *Jachin and Boaz* (1762)."

During his lifetime, Webb constantly improved, refined, and expanded his *Monitor*. Webb's purpose was to promote, assist, and educate the fledgling American Masonic movement. By the time of his death in 1819, his book had run through seven editions.

In addition to systematizing the Blue Lodge ritual, Webb's work also formed the foundation for what is considered "standard" American Masonic Ritual. This includes the American Masonic system of Chapters and Encampments, "the York Rite (Royal Arch, Cryptic or the Council of Royal & Select Masters, and the Knights Templar)," i.e., Chapter, Council, and Commandery.

Webb's work was later expanded and propagated by Jeremy Ladd Cross, John Barney, and other itinerant Masonic lecturers during the early nineteenth century. In 1819, Jeremy L. Cross (1783-1861), "a pupil of Thomas Smith Webb," published *The True Masonic Chart or Hieroglyphic Monitor.* In this work, Cross borrowed liberally from the previous work of Webb. In fact, Cross' *Chart* is—in nearly all its parts—a mere transcript of Webb's *Monitor* (1797). Arturo de Hoyos notes that Cross' *True Masonic Chart or Hieroglyphic Monitor* was "the first Masonic monitor to include illustrations." These engravings and illustrations were an entirely new and original feature. In practice, these illustrations provided useful memory aids to ritualists. As a result, during the first half of the nineteenth century, the Cross monitor became very popular among the Brethren. In fact, for a time, it actually superseded Webb's *Monitor.*

Thus, the genealogy of American Masonic ritual goes from William Preston's *Illustrations of Masonry* (1772), to Thomas Smith Webb's *Monitor* (1797), to Jeremy L. Cross' *The True Masonic Chart or Hieroglyphic Monitor* (1819).

Perhaps the most interesting and useful edition of Webb's *Freemason's Monitor* was published by John Sherer and Rob Morris in 1861. Famous for its beautiful and classic illustrations, copies of this edition can often be found in the back closets and storage areas of our older Masonic Temples.

Second, throughout his exhaustive and definitive biography of Thomas Smith Webb, author Herbert T. Leyland (1898-1966) repeatedly refers to Webb as "the Founding Father." Indeed, due to his "fervency and zeal," combined with his charismatic personality and natural leadership and organizational skills, Thomas Smith Webb is indeed the founder of the system of work which is generally referred to as "the York Rite."

Cornelius Moore explains that, "when Mr. Webb entered the Mystic Temple as a novice, he found it in disorder. Some of the parts were incomplete, some were rudely constructed, others were out of place, and some were wanting." Prior to Thomas Smith Webb, early American Freemasonry had little if any unity in the work. While the essentials were the same, specific ritual variations were enormous. Some of the lodges had been influenced by the conflict between the Antient and Modern Freemasons back in England, while other lodges in America were doing patchwork variations of French, Scottish, and Irish rituals. To all of this, creative local "work" made for a veritable ritual hodge-podge and mish-mash throughout various early American jurisdictions.

Among Masonic scholars, "it is generally conceded that Webb arranged and systematized the degrees pertaining to the Chapter into the Encampment." Webb "doubtlessly found the whole series in fragments, and scattered abroad, without form, system, or harmony." He carefully "gathered up the parts, and arranged them into a complete [and coherent] whole."

Moore adds that at the time Thomas Smith Webb settled in "Albany, New York (i.e., 1793), that city was a great Masonic center." From Albany, Webb "aided in organizing a Chapter and Encampment, and the degrees of the York Rite were worked from Entered Apprentice through all the degrees of Symbolic, Capitular, and Chivalric Masonry up to the Knights of Malta."

Indeed, for this reason, Thomas Smith Webb is rightfully called the "Founding Father of the York [or American Rite]."

THREE: Following the lead of Herbert T. Leyland, Thomas Smith Webb's life can be described and divided into three parts: Entrepreneur, Freemason, and Musician. Leyland adds that without question, during his lifetime, "he earned all three of these titles."

Entrepreneur

Thomas Smith Webb was born in Boston, Massachusetts, on October 30, 1771. By an interesting coincidence, Albert Pike was also born in Boston, Massachusetts. Albert Pike (1809-1891), who, much like Thomas Smith Webb had done for the York Rite, rewrote, reorganized, and recreated the Scottish Rite ritual. Pike was an explorer, a schoolteacher, a writer, a poet, a musician, a newspaper editor and publisher, a philosopher, an attorney, a judge, a Confederate officer, and above all, a Freemason. Pike spent his childhood in Byfield and Newburyport, Massachusetts. He attended school in Newburyport and Framingham, Massachusetts, until he was 15. In August 1825, he passed the entrance exams at Harvard University. When the college requested payment of tuition fees for the first two years, which he had successfully challenged by examination, he chose not to attend. Thus, Pike began a lifelong program of self-education. In 1831, Pike left Massachusetts to travel West to seek his fortune.

Webb received his formal education at the rigorous Boston Latin School. Boston Latin was founded in 1634. It is the first and oldest public school in America. Traditionally, graduates of Boston Latin went on to Harvard. According to the Rev. Paul Dean, Webb entered the Boston Latin School in July of 1779 at the age of 7 years and 9 months. Leyland explains that boys who attended the Boston Latin School learned "under stern and businesslike discipline." The school term lasted for the entire year, and the school day ran from 7:00 AM until 5:00 PM six days a week (Sunday exempted). Among other things, the curriculum focused on the classics in the original Greek and Latin. According to a *Short Talks Bulletin* profile, "Webb became proficient in French and Latin as well as his mother tongue. He was a rare combination of poet, dreamer, visionary, and practical man of action, having much of the mental equipment and character development which has been the foundation of inspired leadership throughout the world's history." Moore adds that at Boston Latin, "Webb made rapid progress, and became an excellent scholar." Also, during this time of his life, he began the serious study of poetry and music which provided an enjoyable diversion throughout his life.

Webb graduated from Boston Latin School in July of 1786 at the age of 14. From here, rather than going on to Harvard or another college, young Webb began serving an apprenticeship in his father's printing and bookbinding shop. Leyland explains that "in eighteenth-century Boston bookselling and bookbinding went hand-in-hand. Bookselling also included the sale of stationery and articles classed as office supplies, such as ink powder, quill pens, sealing wax, etc."

In New England, at the time, apprenticeships typically lasted seven years [from the ages of 14 to 21]. However, apparently due to his previous experience working with his father, Thomas Smith Webb's apprenticeship only lasted four years. He completed his apprenticeship in the Spring or early Summer of 1790.

In America, printing in the late eighteenth-century was the equivalent of the Information Age [computer technology] in the late twentieth-century. It is not an accident that the early American printing industry tended to attract the best and the brightest.

For example, Benjamin Franklin (1705-1790) [also born in Boston, Massachusetts], first made his mark in the world as a printer's apprentice and then finally as a printer in Philadelphia, Pennsylvania.

Like Benjamin Franklin—and later Albert Pike—Thomas Smith Webb was essentially a self-educated man. While his formal schooling ended at age 14 when he graduated from Boston Latin, all of his life Webb was a prolific reader. Among the texts that he read, Webb carefully studied *Blackstone's Commentaries on the Law*. Leyland notes that, "a four-volume edition of *Blackstone's Commentaries* was sold at the auction of Webb's effects. Other law books also were sold." As a result, he was worthy and well-qualified to serve on various committees that drafted the new constitutions for all three York Rite bodies.

Apparently, Thomas Smith Webb was a restless soul willing to relocate in an attempt to improve his entrepreneurial and business prospects. In 1790, after completing his apprenticeship, Webb moved to the village of Keene, New Hampshire. At the time, Keene had a population of 300. It the end of the eighteenth-century, Western Mass and the upper Connecticut River Valley appeared to be the land of opportunity. After less than two years, in 1792, Webb moved back to Boston. In early 1793, he relocated once again to become involved in "the paper staining business [wallpaper manufacturing]" with a partner in Hartford, Connecticut.

Later in 1793, Webb moved to Albany, New York. In Albany, he established a bookstore and a paper-staining factory. In 1798, Webb relocated to Providence, Rhode Island. Leyland explains that in addition to business reasons, Webb chose Providence, Rhode Island, because he "opposed the reactionary opinions of the

Boston Federalists." Throughout his life, Webb was a Jeffersonian Democrat-Republican.

In Providence, he operated a bookstore and continued in the wallpaper business. Webb also became an agent for the Hope Cotton Company. From Providence, Webb moved to Walpole, Massachusetts, where he established a cotton factory. This factory was one of the first in the nation to employ safety devices to protect the life and limbs of employees. In 1817, due to the bad economy [economic dislocation from *The Napoleonic Wars* and the *War of 1812*], he moved his factory to Worthington, Ohio, a suburb of Columbus.

Thus, throughout his life he moved from Boston to Keene, New Hampshire; back to Boston; to Hartford, Connecticut; then to Albany, New York; then to Providence, Rhode Island; then Walpole, Massachusetts [thirteen miles from Boston]; and ultimately out "West" to Ohio, where he died suddenly. One of the benefits of being an operative "traveling man" was that Thomas Smith Webb built a firm network of loyal friends and associates wherever he went. Ultimately, this network helped him as he organized and spread York Rite Masonry.

In addition to Freemasonry, Webb was very involved in civic affairs. During his stay in Rhode Island, he was elected to the school committee, became a director of the Providence Library Company, and served as a director, trustee, and finally treasurer of the Providence Mutual Fire Insurance Company. From the rank of private in the State Militia, Webb rose to the rank of Colonel in his regiment. As a result, in his many biographical profiles, he is referred to as "Col. Webb."

Musician

From his early school days, Thomas Smith Webb enjoyed singing sacred music. He had an excellent tenor singing voice. He also composed several Masonic odes. His musical attainments were considerable, and he was the first president of *The Psallonian Society*. In 1815, having changed his residence to Boston, he instituted, in connection with others, *The Handel and Haydn Society*. Webb served as the first president. *The Handel and Haydn Society*, an American chorus and period instrument orchestra based in Boston, Massachusetts, remains one of the oldest performing arts organizations in the United States.

The Handel and Haydn Society was founded as an oratorio society that hoped to bring Boston audiences the best of the old (Handel) and new (Haydn) in concerts of the highest artistic quality. *The Society's* premier performance was on Christmas Eve in 1815 at King's Chapel in Boston, with a chorus of ninety men and ten women.

The Handel and Haydn Society performed a concert for President [and Brother] James Monroe (1758-1831) on July 5, 1817, in the First Congregational Church in Boston on Chauncey Place. During this gala concert, Thomas Smith Webb served as conductor. Interestingly, on the same "good-will" visit to the Boston area—on July 12, 1817—President Monroe visited Newburyport, Massachusetts. As a young schoolboy Albert Pike recalled with pride seeing the President.

During its history, *The Handel and Haydn Society* has given a number of notable American premieres, including Handel's *Messiah* in 1818, Haydn's *The Creation* in 1819, and Verdi's *Requiem* in 1878. Since 1854, *The Society* has continued annual renditions of Georg Friedrich Handel's *Messiah.*

Freemason

While living in Keene, New Hampshire, Thomas Smith Webb was made a Mason in Rising Sun Lodge on December 24, 1790. *Mackey's Masonic Encyclopedia* states that "when and where Webb received the advanced Degrees has not been stated, but we find him, while living at Albany, engaged in the establishment of a Chapter and an Encampment." Moore, quoting the Rev. Paul Dean's *Eulogy*, states that it is likely that Webb had at some point earlier received his advanced Degrees in Philadelphia. Leyland states that, "on a visit to Philadelphia, Webb received the most sublime degree of Royal Arch Mason on May 18, 1796."

In 1796, at the age of 26, Webb assisted in the founding of Temple Lodge in Albany. He served as Temple Lodge's first Senior Warden. He was also instrumental in founding both the Chapter and Temple Encampment in 1797. He served as High Priest of the Chapter. In 1798, after moving to Providence, Rhode Island, he became active with Freemasonry. He joined Providence Royal Arch Chapter October 11, 1799. In February 1801, he signed the Bylaws of St. Johns Lodge. In June, 1802, he was elected Junior Grand Warden of Grand Lodge. On August 11, 1802, along with five others, Webb established St. Johns Commandery No. 1 of Providence. In 1803 he was elected Senior Grand Warden, and in 1813, he was elected Grand Master of Freemasons for the State of Rhode Island. On October 24, 1797, "a Convention of Committees from several Royal Arch Chapters in the Northern States met in Boston for the purpose of deliberating on the propriety and expediency of establishing a Grand

Chapter of Royal Arch Masons for the Northern States." At this convention, Thomas Smith Webb was chosen as the chairman.

Apparently, prior to 1797, Royal Arch Degrees had been conferred in Masters Lodges under a Lodge Warrant. Under the influence of Webb Royal Arch Chapters were disentangled from the Blue Lodge and established as independent Chapters. According to *Mackey's Masonic Encyclopedia,* "this was one of the first steps involved in the systematic organization of the York Rite." As a result, the General Grand Chapter was organized in January 1798. At this point, Webb was elected General Grand Scribe. He was reelected in 1799, when the Body officially assumed the title of "General Grand Chapter."

In 1806, Webb was elected to the office of General Grand King. In 1816, he graciously deferred to DeWitt Clinton (1769-1828), who was elected General Grand High Priest in his place. Webb then became Deputy General Grand High Priest. He held this position until his death.

In 1816, Webb traveled to the Western States for business. He remained there for two years. During this time, he actively engaged in the establishment and organization of Chapters, Grand Chapters, and Encampments. By virtue of his powers as a General Grand Officer, Webb established the Grand Chapters of Ohio and Kentucky.

The One Death and Three Burials of TSW

FOUR: The "four" in Thomas Smith Webb's life is his sudden death at the age of 48 and his thrice-burial. One of the odd things about Thomas Smith Webb is that—like our Grand Master Hiram—he received *three* burials.

On July 6, 1819, while on a business trip in Cleveland, Ohio,

Thomas Smith Webb died suddenly of "a fit of apoplexy [i.e., a stroke or a cerebral hemorrhage]." Reportedly, following the attack that proved to be fatal, attending doctors—following prescribed medical procedures of the day—bled him from the arm and the temple. Samuel Cowls, in a letter to a mutual friend back in Boston wrote, "I think his friends may be satisfied that all was done that could be done to save him. At any rate, there was no want of goodwill or exertions on the part of physicians and others."

Leyland, in a discussion of the cause of Webb's death writes that several factors contributed to his untimely demise. First, Webb was exceedingly worried over his financial affairs. Because of the *Panic of 1819*, he lost a large part of his life savings. *The Panic* led to the second major financial blow that Webb experienced within a four-year period [the first was a consequence of major economic dislocations related to the *War of 1812*].

In addition, "in common with most of his contemporaries, Webb typically worked fifteen to eighteen hours daily (except Sundays)." Indeed, Webb was a hard-driving man interested in many things [business, Freemasonry, community service, and sacred music], and he was driven to succeed in all of them.

Also, writes Leyland, the combination of "worry, improper diet, and insufficient rest and exercise combined to impair the circulatory apparatus." If Thomas Smith Webb were alive today, undoubtedly, doctors would be treating him with anti-anxiety and blood pressure medication.

His first burial occurred within twenty-four hours of his death in Cleveland, Ohio. Moore states that "the remains of Col. Webb were buried in Cleveland... with Masonic honors, and the craft throughout the country deeply mourned his sudden and unexpected decease. He was in the prime of life, being not quite forty-eight years of age; was the best ritualist in America, and was universally beloved for his excellent qualities, by all who knew him."

When news of Webb's death reached Boston, his many friends organized a memorial service. On August 19, 1819, at the request of the Masonic, Handel and Haydn, and Philharmonic Societies, a public memorial service was held in Boylston Hall in Boston. The Rev. Paul Dean led the service and delivered the eulogy. The Rev. Paul Dean, a personal friend of Thomas Smith Webb, was a well-respected Trinitarian-Universalist minister in Boston. Like many prominent early Universalists in Boston, Dean was an active Freemason. From 1814 to 1836 Paul Dean served as Grand Chaplain of the Grand Lodge of Massachusetts and Chaplain of the Columbian Lodge. In 1837, Rev. Paul Dean was elected Grand Master of the Grand Lodge of Massachusetts. He was the first clergyman elected to that office in Massachusetts.

His Masonic friends in Providence, Rhode Island, felt that he should be buried with honors in Rhode Island. Thus, his mortal remains—placed in a large packing case filled with lime mortar—were removed for re-internment on November 8, 1819, in the West Burying Ground in Providence.

In 1862, forty-three years after his death, because his original tomb had fallen into disrepair and the West Burying Ground had been essentially abandoned and neglected, Freemasons formed the Webb Monument Association, which raised funds for a re-interment and an appropriate monument. Thus, Thomas Smith Webb was reinterred with Masonic honors in the North Burial Ground in Providence, Rhode Island. At the new plot, an impressive marble monument or obelisk was erected by the Grand Lodge of Rhode Island. Each side of the shaft was used to record one or more of his many accomplishments. Thus, "the remains of this brilliant Freemason are interred in the North Burial Ground... where an unpretentious memorial erected by the Grand Lodge bears witness to the fame and usefulness of this indefatigable laborer in the quarries."

Thomas Smith Webb is buried in the North Burial Ground in Providence, Rhode Island

Bibliography

Abbott, Norris G. Jr. "Founding Father of the York Rite." Northern Light, Vol. 2, No. 1. (January 1971).

Bailyn, Bernard, editor. "The Debate on the Constitution: Federalist and Anti-Federalist Speeches, Articles, and Letters During the Struggle Over Ratification". New York: Library of America, 1993.

Blackstone, William. "Commentaries on the Laws of England". Oxford, Clarendon Press, 1765–1769.

Brands, H.W. "The First American: The Life and Times of Benjamin Franklin". New York: Doubleday, 2000.

Brown, Walter Lee. "A Life of Albert Pike". Fayetteville, AK: University of Arkansas Press, 1997.

Condon, R. M. C. Thomas Smith Webb: Masonic Ritualist. "The Builder". The National Masonic Research Society (October, 1918).

Cross, Jeremy L. "The True Masonic Chart or Hieroglyphic Monitor". New York: Robert B. Collins, 1819, 1851.

de Hoyos, Arturo. "Light on Masonry: The History of Rituals of America's Most Important Masonic Expose". Washington, D.C.: Scottish Rite Research Society, 2008.

Dean, Paul. *A Eulogy Delivered in Boylston Hall, Boston at the Request of the Masonic, Handel and Haydn, and Philharmonic Societies, August 19, 1819, on the Character of Their Late Friend and Brother Thomas Smith Webb, Esq.*

Ferling, John. "Adams vs. Jefferson: The Tumultuous Election of 1800". New York: Oxford University Press, 2004.

Hamilton, Alexander, John Jay, and James Madison. *The Federalist Papers.* New York: The Modern Library, 1787-1788, 2000.

Hodapp, Christopher. "Freemasonry for Dummies". Hoboken, N.J.: Wiley Publishing, Inc., 2005.

Leyland, Herbert T. "Thomas Smith Webb: Freemason, Musician, Entrepreneur". Dayton, Ohio: The Otterbein Press, 1965.

Mackey, Albert G. "Encyclopedia of Freemasonry and Kindred

Sciences: New Edition Revised and Enlarged". New York: Masonic History Company, 1929.

Moore, Cornelius. *Leaflets of Masonic Biography: or Sketches of Eminent Freemasons.* Cincinnati Ohio: The Masonic Review Office, 1863, 2012.

Pike, Albert. Edited by Arturo de Hoyos, "Morals and Dogma of the Ancient and Accepted Scottish Rite of Freemasonry: Annotated Edition". Washington, D.C. The Supreme Council Ancient and Accepted Scottish Rite of Freemasonry, Southern Jurisdiction, 1872, 2011.

Pike, Albert. Edited by Arturo de Hoyos. "Albert Pike's Esoterika: Symbolism of the Blue Degrees of Freemasonry". Washington, D.C.: Scottish Rite Research Society.

Rothbard, Murray N. "The Panic of 1819". Literary Licensing, LLC, 1962, 2011.

Roy, Thomas Sherrard. "Stalwart Builders: A History of the Grand Lodge of Massachusetts, 1733 – 1970". Boston: The Masonic Education and Charity Trust of the Grand Lodge of Massachusetts, 1971.

Tabbert, Mark A. "American Freemasons". New York: New York University Press, 2005.

Toffler, Alvin. "The Third Wave". New York: William Morrow and Co., 1980.

Tresner, James T. "Albert Pike: The Man Beyond the Monument". New York: M. Evans and Co., 1995.

Webb, Thomas Smith. "Freemason's Monitor or Illustrations of Masonry". Reprint. New York: Masonic Historical Society of New York, 1791, 1896.

4

The Passing of the Veils

MARK Z. OLDKNOW

Good morning. A new day! And an especially appropriate time to approach this morning's topic: the veils encountered in the Holy Royal Arch degree and the esoteric meaning of the ritual act of "Passing the Veils". Each dawn offers a moment that symbolizes our awakening, a passing from a state of sleep and dream to a state of (relative) awareness and clarity. In that moment of budding into the new day we are "becoming", we are potential ready to happen, neither yet being or not. In the Blue Lodge, the Worshipful Master is even likened to the Sun rising in the east, symbolizing the great work of Masonry. As we start this esoteric presentation, perhaps it's not surprising to observe that one of the most influential of hermetic societies is publicly known as the Order of the Golden Dawn, and was established as such by three Masonic Rosicrucians in London in the early 1880s. But that's another presentation...

I've already referred to this an esoteric topic and it's worth pausing in advance to be clear about what that means. The word esoteric refers simply to truth that is reserved for someone who has the privilege. It does not necessarily mean that something esoteric is hidden or secret, and certainly the term should not be confused with occult, which does refer to a truth shadowed or hidden behind something else. In our context and for our purposes today, esoteric is simply something made available to the initiate. Once a man has crossed the threshold of the Lodge or Chapter, Council or Conclave, he has symbolically embarked on a new personal beginning. He is an initiate. He is entitled to certain information not available to the profane, but more especially he has earned a new perspective on his symbols, his world, and himself. The esoteric is simply the quality of seeing through that fresh perspective. It's not secret. In fact, it is often quite "out in the open". Sometimes the best way to protect and preserve something is to hide it in clear sight, very much reserved for those with the eyes to see and ears to hear.

Having said that, the ritual act of "passing the veils" is an ancient symbol adopted and adapted by Royal Arch Masonry. Perhaps second only to the core story itself of the Loss and Recovery of the Word, the passing of the veils is one of the oldest vestiges of the mysteries preserved by Masonry. It is a rich and complex symbol that has meaning in a biblical context, an esoteric context, and a Masonic context. Let's start by looking at the literal meaning of the word "veil". In English, it derives from the Latin *velum* a curtain or sheet as a verb it means to conceal or partition something. But to veil a thing suggests something more subtle than just hiding it. To "reveal" literally means to "veil" again. Indeed, a veil placed over something otherwise invisible does not conceal it, but rather paradoxically serves to reveal its hidden form. Like the all-but-spooky toddler draped under a sheet on Halloween.

As a traditional symbol, the veil communicates a process of revelation and is a seal of initiation. The birth caul, a membrane sometimes draping the fetal head, was appreciated for centuries as a curtain of creation, serving mysteriously to cordon the emerging newborn from the void. Likewise, the veil traditionally partitions the seeker from the sought, the lover from the beloved (for example, the Jewish yarmulke). It is a symbol of discretion and modesty (the Islamic veil) but ultimately also of exposé (the bridal veil). It conveys the sweet seduction and the forbidden mystery of revelation, its vision, and the great quest in its pursuit.

In a biblical context, the veil served an important role in the structure and significance of both the Tabernacle and Solomon's Temple. Both edifices had distinct levels by which a qualified worshipper progressed deeper into the symbolic mysteries and closer to the manifest Presence of YHVH: an outer court, an inner court or adytum, and the Sanctum Sanctorum which housed the Ark of the Covenant. "And thou shalt make a veil of blue and purple and scarlet and fine-twined linen, of cunning work: with cherubims shall it be made: and thou shalt hang it upon four pillars of shittim wood, overlaid with gold: their hooks shall be of gold upon the four sockets of silver" (Ex. 26:31, 32). "He made the veil of blue and purple, and crimson, and fine linen and wrought cherubims thereon" (Chron. 3:14). There are different interpretations of where veils were placed in each edifice, but the typical rendering describes three veils. The first separated the outer court from the sacred space inside, and was always drawn open to all Jewish worshippers. The second separated the outer sanctum from the inner or adytum; it is said to have traditionally been drawn open for all to see inside, but only the priests could actually enter. These first two veils were white. The third veil separated the Inner Sanctum from the Holy of Holies. This veil was only parted once a year, on the Day of Atonement, and only opened enough for the High Priest alone to enter. This veil was colored in hues of Tyrian Purple with the cherubim depicted upon it.

It was necessary to "pass the veils" as one advanced deeper into the House of the Lord and closer to His Presence. The first veil was open and welcomed all true worshippers to enter the porch or inner court. The common man could not pass further inside, although a glimpse of the inner adytum was permitted and symbolically beckoned to those more qualified as initiates and Priests. In the original Tabernacle and Temple, the veils of the outer courts were always open and allowed line-of-sight visibility into those levels. But the final veil that separated the Holy of Holies was kept drawn. It was open only to the highest initiate alone, the High Priest who possessed special knowledge of the Sacred Name of God. It was parted once a year, on the Day of Atonement, by the High Priest as he entered before the Ark and the Shekinah. The Royal Arch Initiate symbolically performs the same. In Christian esotericism, it is taught that the coming of Christ heralded a "rending of the veils", a permanent parting of the veil separating God and creation. The ritual act of passing the veils symbolizes that gradual progression toward a direct knowledge and experience of the mysteries. It is a symbol of the process of initiation itself, the gradual but progressive development and integration of the initiate's own wisdom and abilities.

"Initiation is the ritualized marking of a new beginning in life, and hence is often symbolized as a doorway or threshold that the initiate passes. The veil, in its simplest sense, is just such an initiatory threshold. As a symbol of the initiatory process the ritual act of "Passing the Veils" reflects the gradual development of the Initiate. The layers of the Tabernacle and Temple, and the limitations placed on who was allowed to enter each, show how this is a progression from the common "outer" courts to the select "innermost" sanctum.

Initiation is a very personal experience, but is also shared. As indicated in the Most Excellent Master Mason Degree, and elaborated upon in its corresponding lecture, while they were wandering in the desert God decreed that the Jewish people commemorate their deliverance from Egypt with the seven day Feast of Sukkoth held in the seventh month of Tishrei (Leviticus 23:43). When the Jews left Egypt, God shielded them with "Clouds of Glory" to protect them from the elements. The word Tishrei is derived from the Babylonian meaning "to begin", while the Twelve Tribes of Israel occupied specific localities within the vast kingdoms defined by the Jordan River and Valley. The Temple in Jerusalem was in the locale of the tribe of Benjamin which, in turn, was nearly surrounded by the bordering patriarchies of Judah to the south, Reuben to the east, Dan to the west, and Ephraim to the north. The four Royal Arch veils correspond, among other attributions, to these four tribes that encompassed Jerusalem and the Temple. The Royal Arch initiate symbolically makes a cross centered on Jerusalem by passing the veils in order: the first and second veils form a horizontal-latitudinal arm from in the west to Reuben in the east, the third and fourth veils form the vertical-longitudinal bar from Ephraim in the north, and finally to Judah in the South. This traditional esoteric symbolism extends the meaning of passing the veils: the cross formed upon the symbolic geography of the Holy Land represents the Candidate's own spiritual development. In all its forms, the cross symbolizes balance and integration, the process of achieving harmony between the conflicting elemental forces within each man's soul.

These forces are in turn represented by the four cherubim or animals depicted on the veils. The state of being in harmony or balance is a prerequisite to the focus and discipline needed to open the door of spiritual practice (in my opinion, the most technically savvy and rewarding method available to the modern initiate is the Buddhist practice of *shamatha*, a sort of focused relaxation, which is coupled with and advances the practice of vipasyana or awareness). Let's examine the esoteric symbolism of each veil, and the meaning of its corresponding elemental force, in a bit more detail.

Veil	*Color*	*Animal*	*Tribe*	*Zodiacal Sign*	*Direction*	*Element*	*Alchemical Reference*	*Ritual Instrument*
1st	Blue	Eagle	Dan	Scorpio	West	Water	Purification	Cup
2nd	Violet	Man	Reuben	Aquarius	East	Air	Solution/ Analysis	Dagger
3rd	Scarlet	Ox	Ephraim	Taurus	North	Earth	Coagulation/ Synthesis	Disc or Seal
4th	White	Lion	Judah	Leo	South	Fire	Consecration	Wand

Each Royal Arch veil is similarly arranged: it depicts an animal and the name of a Tribe of Israel set against a solid-colored background. There are four veils in total. The number four esoterically expresses manifestation and concrete reality; it is expresses the four cardinal directions. The four animals are "cherubim", the plural form of the Hebrew word *cherub*, which has older Sumerian roots meaning "mighty" or "blessed". The Cherubim have a rich symbolic history (e.g., Genesis 3, 24; Ezekiel 10; Exodus 25, 20 & 37, 9; 1 Kings 6, 32; 2 Chronicles 5, 8; Hebrews 9, 5). They represent great forces and are traditionally described as an order of angelic beings. They are said to be the keepers or guardians of the very Throne of God.

Indeed, the Ark of the Covenant itself was encompassed by the spread wings of two great cherubim upon its cap, and the Shekinah, or Presence of God, was said to manifest between their joined wings. These two cherubim were traditionally depicted in the Sumerian fashion as a blending of four distinct animals — the lion, ox, eagle, and man. On the Royal Arch banners, these four animals are divided and depicted separately, in effect drawing out the details of the more complex symbol.

In Royal Arch Masonry, the first veil is colored the blue of water. Life on Earth may have been spawned in the primordial oceans, and certainly began to evolve its myriad varieties there. Water has many unusual physical properties that make it a foundation for life indeed a requirement so far as we know (e.g., due to the way it crystallizes, water in its solid form as ice is LESS dense than in its liquid form and so ice floats and forms on the surface of a body of water; if this were not so, the ocean floor would freeze in winter and life would have had little sustained opportunity to evolve). From this perspective, water is the natural "starting place" for the would-be initiate. In the alchemical traditions, as well as in ritual contexts across many cultures, water serves to purify. It cleanses the external soiling of the initiate, the dust which has accumulated and dims the otherwise radiant spirit. It is symbolic of primitive and chaotic emotions that must be focused and trained to energize the spirit, and not to overwhelm, cloud, or occupy it. As such, the element of water is, in turn, symbolized by the cup or grail and the human heart. It is ascribed to the Tribe of Dan and hence to the westerly cardinal direction (in Jewish reckoning, the new day began from sunset). Water is ascribed to the zodiacal sign of Scorpio, the sign astrologically associated with water. Each of the veils is associated with a zodiacal sign, and each

of these with the FIXED expression of one of the classical elements. The "fixed" signs of the zodiac express the invariable nature of the elements rather than their "cardinal" (creative) or "mutable"(adaptive or conjoint) aspects. Fixed signs express elemental forces that act to preserve and maintain the spirit and the world. The symbols upon each banner also have ancient astrological associations with the fixed zodiacal signs and their elemental expression. The symbol upon the first banner is not a Scorpion, but rather an Eagle, a bird well known as a skilled fisher and flyer.

The Initiate is allowed entrance to the 1st Veil in part by dint of sharing the same word gained by Moses from the burning bush. In transliterated Hebrew, this is rendered AHIH AShR AHIH and is appropriately translated in the future tense as SI will be what I will be an apropos key for the new Initiate as he enters into formal spiritual development. The Master of the 1st Veil teaches the lessons of water to the Initiate through certain words and signs. Two of the three sons of Noah hid his nakedness; in effect, they veiled him while the third is traditionally said to have been father to the generations of humankind that arose following the flood. The Master of the 1st Veil then also communicates a parable that reflects Moses' initial emotional state, fear and apprehension of the very rod that God teaches him to hold as an instrument of his power and authority.

Having mastered the lessons of Water in the First Veil, the Initiate advances next to the Second Veil. This veil is colored purple, a mixture of the blue which precedes it and the red which follows because it partakes of both the qualities of these bordering veils. It is the deepening color of the sky at twilight and is associated with the element of Air. Like water, the atmosphere is another, more rarified, ocean. Air symbolizes the analytic mind, the power of the intellect. Although in some ways more focused than the raw and untamed emotions alone, the mind itself must be tamed and tasked. Much of the time the mind "chatters" away on its own accord, throwing up unsolicited thoughts, associations, and reactions. It only requires a basic attempt at stilling the "rude and unpolished" mind to realize just how little it is actually under our conscious control. It is almost as if our thoughts think themselves in and out of our consciousness. But the mind must be yoked if the Initiate is indeed determined to progress upon the path and pass to the next veil. The symbolic working tools of the Mark Master Mason degree speak clearly to this part of the work. In almost all mystical traditions, the breath of God (Greek: *pnuema*, Hebrew: *ruach*) animates the Spirit, and in many yoga practices, the breath is used to quiet and focus the body and mind. In its highest expression, breath is necessary to pronounce the Word. The second veil is attributed to the zodiacal sign Aquarius, which is symbolized by a Human Figure, specifically a Water Carrier. It is classically associated with the ritual knife or dagger, an instrument used to cut or separate. The dagger is like the analytic mind which identifies, labels, and categorizes all that it encounters, which, in its higher expression, becomes the basis for objective knowledge and the law that governs relationships between objects. It is ascribed to the East, the direction of the rising Sun that divides night and day. The Master of the 2nd Veil communicates to the Initiate words that reflect the Law of God: the names of the one who received the Ten Commandments, but also the overseers in charge of the weaving of the veils and the forging of the brass instruments from which they were hung. The initiate receives a parable that teaches the symbol of the clean and unclean hand, the hand being the part of the body that enacts what the mind thinks.

With these words and symbols, the Initiate passes to the third veil. It is colored scarlet, and is associated with elemental Earth and the zodiacal sign of Taurus. Its color reminds us of blood, which the ancients (in part correctly) understood to carry the vital energy throughout the body. Indeed, the color scarlet-red has long association in the West with the passions, especially with lust. Its lesson, therefore, is control of the physical body, characterized by fortitude and perseverance, which is dependent upon first gaining some facility at control of the heart and mind. Note that the body is not considered base, it is actually an expression, even a result, of the preceding faculties (herein is a truly Greater Mystery to be elucidated elsewhere). Under the discipline of the yoke, the power of the Ox clears and furrows the earth preparing it for planting. It is ascribed to the North, the apparent direction the Sun travels as its light increases and as plants grow (in the northern hemisphere, of course). The Master of the 3rd Veil communicates the names of the members of the Grand Council, names symbolizing earthly authority and the Great Work that the Council oversees. He also recounts a parable that, in part describes water becoming blood i.e. a summary and proof of the Initiate's passage so far). The ritual instrument ascribed to Earth is the Coin or Wheel, conveying a sense of tangible purchase and motion, but more generally by any circle – the geometric symbol of perfection, of the dimensionless point extended in to physical manifestation. The Master of the 3rd Veil then presents the Initiate with a ring-a form of a circle as a Signet or Seal of Authority, for the Initiate has now demonstrated symbolically that he has control over the three classical parts of his existence: heart or soul, mind or psyche, and body. As an aside, the Royal Arch Degree requires three yoked candidates to proceed together; in turn, these also reflect the same three classical constituent parts of each Initiate himself.

Finally, with these lessons and with the Signet, the Initiate passes to the fourth and final veil. It is colored white and symbolizes the Spirit itself, that nexus point of Divine Presence in each person. The emblem on the Fourth Veil is the Lion of Judah, the tribe with which it is associated. It is astrologically attributed to the sign of Leo (the Lion) and to the classical element of fire. Here the Initiate is prepared to take the final steps that will advance him to the presence of the Grand Council. In its simplest expression, the classical element of fire is an aspect of light. Indeed, the sign of Leo is said to be astrologically "ruled" by the Sun itself. In higher expression, fire serves the ritual purpose of consecration. Consecration is the act of making or reserving something as sacred. It is a higher form of the ritual act of purification that the Initiate passed in the first veil and elemental water. But consecration does not simply wash away an outer coating of dust, but rather serves to "burn away" internal impurities. By the sheer purity of its remaining essence, symbolized by the white color of the final veil, the consecrated object becomes focused, dedicated, and balanced.

The signet or ring has a very special esoteric significance. It is the Signet of Zerubabel, the Prince of the House of Judah, and the seal of his god-given authority. Rings are ancient symbols of union, still celebrated with the exchange of wedding rings. An ancient method of establishing proof or authority was to break a signet and divide the halves between two persons who, when they reconvened at some later date or distant location, would compare the two halves to prove their union, identity, and authority. This broken signet was called a "symbolon" in Greek and is the root source of the word symbol. Indeed, a symbol serves to connect the mind to a higher meaning, and here the Signet of Zerubabel qualifies the Initiate, who has now passed the veils and symbolically achieved a state of elemental harmony and balance, to advance before the Grand Council. And from there he will be set to work. And, well, his story has really just begun...

5

The Chisel in the Hand of the Skillful Workman

PETER PIZZORNO

{Peter Pizzorno had been a Royal Arch Companion for fourteen years at the time this was presented, and served the Grand Chapter State of New York Royal Arch Masons as its Grand Lecturer.}

This paper is intended to be the first in a series dealing with the centrality of Ritual in a life led Masonically. These papers are to be a mixture of considered opinion and traditional research and reference. Their purpose is to focus on Ritual as the defining aspect of who we are as Masons and how this conscious focus is the essential step in any success we may hope to have in personal Masonic growth and social Masonic activity. They will even go as far as to suggest that without the primacy of the lessons taught by Ritual informing, i.e., giving form to, our actions, any attempts to repair the deficiencies of the Fraternity and strengthen the craft will probably fail.

This paper sets up the parameters and topography of this process. It is a research document in that it rests upon the linguistic roots of the word "research". Here research is understood as a seeking again and again after meaning and understanding. It has its base in the deep personal interest of the seeker who then shares his data, interpretations, and reflections with others of similar interests. He then uses their reactions, comments, etc. as a spur to further research and understanding. In this way, intellectual solipsism is avoided and personal growth encouraged and achieved. Furthermore, this idea of research is a fundamental Masonic activity. As the Keystone Lecture states:

The design of all Masonry is a search for truth and he who earnestly seeks it shall be rewarded for his labors in the attainment of his desires.

In the Academia Gallery of Florence, Italy, is Michelangelo's masterpiece, David. As one enters the gallery, its placement immediately draws attention, so much so that is very easy to pass by a series of sculptures displayed on either side. These works are called *I Prigionieri*, The Prisoners. They are unfinished. However, in that state, the figures seem almost alive, as if struggling to achieve freedom and completeness from the marble in which they are partially encased. This style of artistic endeavor has been called Michelangelo's "Non-Finito", unfinished and never intended to be so. Moreover, according to Michelangelo, the blocks of marble themselves called forth their human shapes. His duty as artist was to listen to this need and uncover what was there. In this way they reflect the continuing and never-ending human struggle to fulfill what we can be.

We all know that one of the Working Tools of a Mark Master Mason is the Chisel. We are received into the MMM Lodge on the edge of the engraver's chiseled and later are told:

The mind, like the rough ashlar, when taken from the quarries is rude and unpolished; but as the effect of the chisel in the hands of a skillful workman soon outlines and perfects the carved capital, the stately shaft, and the beautiful statue so education discovers the latent virtues of the mind and draws them forth to range the large fields of matter and space, to display the summit of human knowledge, our duty to God and man.

I submit that the image and process of I Prigionieri is a reflective symbol of the centrality of Ritual in our Masonic lives:

1. The tool of interaction between the artist and the marble is the Chisel. For us that Chisel is the Ritual. One could argue that, according to the quote above, "education" is central to the process. The question must then be asked upon what this education is based; whence comes its inspiration. For Masons, it has to be ritual.

2. Who are the skillful workmen? Who are the people who use Ritual to interact with the rough Aslar? Who are they that allow the Aslar to take its proper individual shape? It is we Masons. Who are the ashlars from which will emerge a never-ending continuum of personal growth? Again, it is we Masons. Consider the dynamic. Via Ritual, we craft the square stones which will form the Temple of Masonry, while at the same time being

crafted to be those stones. Remember that in the PM Degree the RWM says. **"...I trust that you will prove a square stone in the temple of Masonry."** "Proving" in this context means to demonstrate yourself to be as such, with "trust" emphasizing a certitude that something will be accomplished.

3. There is a synergy in the process. In the case of I Prigionieri, the synergy occurred between the stone, chisel, and Michelangelo, with the stone evoking what it is meant to be and Michelangelo open to its demands via the chisel. In Masonry, this synergy is a much more integrated process with the workman, chisel, and ashlars intimately connected, each needing the other. The chisel of Ritual contains meaning but cannot become meaningful without the interaction and identification of the workman and the living stone. Without the chisel, the workman and living stone remain ill-formed and purposeless.

As regards this last statement concerning the lack of synergy between Ritual, the skilled workman and the living ashlars, one can ask how such a theoretical concept can be verified in practice. After all, there should be discernible evidence of such a breakdown. There is a Paul Simon song that, *Everything Put Together Falls Apart.* Putting together here means not having a strong bond, integration, or synergy of coherence. I would think that in our Fraternity this situation would manifest itself by a decrease of membership, disrespect or sloppiness in Ritual and inattention when it is being presented, disharmony in our Lodges and Chapters, attention and criticism to the faults and motives of others, an inordinate concentration on title, rank and position, the inability of Masonic bodies to consistently provide programs that attract members and encourage their Masonic growth. Unfortunately, I think that we all have seen and experienced too many instances of the above.

In the final analysis, what do we have as Masons that distinguishes us from other groups? We have no catechism of beliefs. No special revelation from above. The Volumes of Sacred Law that we use are borrowed from religions. We are not a religion. What we do have is the synergy that exists between ourselves and the Ritual. It is not a "put together" relationship, but one that to be effective must intimately cohere to the point that consciously and subconsciously all our actions are habitually informed by the lessons and values of Ritual, while at the same time expanding the meaning of that Ritual by our lives as Masons.

6

Hipólito José da Costa

JEFFREY M. WILLIAMSON

{At the time of this presentation, Jeffrey M. Williamson was Deputy General Grand High Priest, Northeast Region, General Grand Chapter Royal Arch Masons International}

This story begins in November of 2011, when we had the opportunity of traveling to São Paulo, Brazil, to attend the 10th Anniversary of the Supreme Grand Chapter of Royal Arch Masons of Brazil. We were officially attending this event in our capacity as an Officer of the General Grand Chapter of Royal Arch Masons International. This was my second trip to this wonderful Grand Jurisdiction and we were responsible to supervise several elements of the program that included conferral of Degrees & Orders, not only in Royal Arch but in Templary as well.

Over the preceding two years, the Sir Knights of Brazil successfully conferred the Order of Red Cross and the Order of Malta upon a class of three hundred candidates (that's right — you heard me!). The challenge now before us was the conferral of the summit of Templary — the Order of the Temple. My role as "Coach" of the Brazilian Team was to instruct the Sir Knights on the proper floor work, tactics, and ritual for the Order of the Temple.

This project proved very successful for the Brazilian Templars, as Sir Knight David Dixon Goodwin, then R.E. Deputy Grand Master of the Grand Encampment of Knights Templar, and Sir Knight Lawrence E. Tucker, R.E. Grand Recorder, were on hand to witness the Order and declared the Brazilian Knights proficient and competent in their conferral of the Templar Orders.

On Sunday, we ended the Grand Sessions, and on Monday, the American delegation hoped to go on a short tour of São Paulo. The Brazilians promptly ordered a van and driver and we ventured forth into the busy city traffic to see some of the sights.

Eventually we arrived at The Monument to the Independence of Brazil, also known as the Altar of the Fatherland. It is an impressive sculpture, set in granite and bronze. It is located on the banks of the Ipiranga Brook, in São Paulo, on the historic site where Pedro I of Brazil proclaimed the independence of the Country on September 7, 1822.

Inside the monument are the Brazilian Imperial Crypt and Chapel. The crypt was built in 1952 to house the remains of Emperor Pedro I of Brazil, also King Pedro IV of Portugal, and his wives, Maria Leopoldina of Austria and Amélie of Leuchtenberg.

As we admired the massive monument, we noticed that situated around the base of the sculpture were various bronze statues of what we assumed were famous Brazilians and Founding Fathers of the country. They were seated on thrones or chairs, and one statue particularly caught my eye. This prompted me to inquire of our good friend, the Most Excellent João Guilherme Ribeiro, Deputy General Grand High Priest of South America, and Past Grand High Priest of Brazil — "Who was the dignitary portrayed on the throne"?

With an almost reverential attitude, he pointed out that the figure was a famous Brazilian journalist, diplomat, and Freemason, and is considered to be the "Father of Brazilian Press", and with that assertion, asked if we could take a picture of him posing next to the statue (which we gladly complied with his request!).

With the seed of curiosity firmly planted in my mind, I returned home with a resolution to know more about this individual who was worthy of this place of honor at one of the most important monuments in the history of Brazil!

Hipólito José da Costa Pereira Furtado de Mendonça (a mouthful, certainly!) is recognized as the *Patron of Brazilian Journalism*, and was undoubtedly one of the foremost builders of Brazilian Independence. But much remains to be found and told about this powerful and ubiquitous Freemason, a moral force behind the Brazilian struggle for freedom. He was a cultured mind in a country made deliberately illiterate. Hipólito was born in 1774 in the old Colony of Sacramento, in what is now Uruguay. When the colony was ceded to the Spaniards, the Costa family emigrated to Rio Grande do Sul, Brazil's Southernmost State.

Hipólito obtained his degree in law at the University of Coimbra, Portugal. He was commissioned by the Portuguese Crown to observe technologies in the United States and Mexico that could be brought to Portugal, like the cochineal insect, used to dye textiles. Hipolito presented detailed reports on tobacco, sugarcane, whale fishing, bridges, yellow fever, public sanitation, the American Navy, and several engineering projects. He traveled a lot, touring several Eastern States and Canada.

It is believed that he was made a Mason when just 25 years old in Philadelphia, at the George Washington Lodge No. 59. He was presented to John Adams and Thomas Jefferson, being quite impressed by the simplicity of American customs, quite different of the stuffiness prevalent in the Portuguese court. His very detailed diary does not mention his Masonic condition, perhaps because of the persecutions of Freemasons in Portugal.

Later in 1800, Hipólito returned to Lisbon and was appointed publisher of the Imprensa Regia (the royal printworks). As such, he was sent to London to buy books for the public library, but also to contact the *Premier Grand Lodge* on behalf of four Portuguese Lodges. William Preston's classic *Illustrations of Masonry* reports Hipolito as the representative of four Portuguese Lodges.

Meanwhile, gossip was rife in Portugal. Hipólito was warned, but nevertheless went back to Lisbon. He was arrested and accused of spreading Masonic ideas through Europe, and it took three years for the Portuguese and English Freemasons to dig him out of the dungeons of the *Holy Office*, the dreaded Inquisition. His report on the Inquisition's abominable ways ranks with John Coustos's. After hiding a year among Portuguese Brethren (who ran a great danger themselves), Hipolito escaped to England.

In 1808, he entered *Antiquity Lodge*, whose Master was the Duke of Sussex, a firm friend and supporter. There he was Deputy Master in 1812-13. The Duke of Sussex, first Grand Master of the new *United Grand Lodge of England*, would be at the helm for some thirty years. Hipolito was his private secretary as long as he lived.

John Hamill, UGLE's Librarian, says that.... "*H.J. da Costa has great importance in Brazilian culture and independence and, as recently found out, no less importance in the development of our rituals immediately before and after the Union of 1813".*

Hipólito was appointed a part of the "Nine Worthies". This was a group of Masons of notable wisdom who were designated by each of the Modern and Antient Grand Lodges to reach consensus on the consolidated rituals of both Rites so they could go forward with the Union project.

Hipólito was a member of both the *Lodge of Promulgation* (1809-1811), who were tasked to rewrite the rituals and the *Lodge of Reconciliation* (1813-1816), which taught the new rituals. Recent research brought forth several of his manuscripts on the new rituals.

The Duke of Sussex also made Hipólito Secretary for Foreign Affairs, Chairman of the Finances Council and Provincial Grand Master of Ruthland (who actually had no Lodges!). Besides that, Hipolito was a very active Royal Arch Mason, being one of two Masons appointed to examine Sussex, when the Duke was installed Grand First Principal. Among his close friends, we find William Preston, the ritualist, and Francisco Miranda, a hero of Venezuela's independence.

But Hipólito did not forget his country and the struggle for independence. From 1808 until Brazilian independence, he wrote, edited, and published the *Correio Braziliense* (Brazilian Courier), also called *Armazém Literário* (Literary Shop), the first Brazilian newspaper, even though printed in England. It was a sensitive and accurate account of the socio-political conditions in Brazil and Portugal and a voice for reforms and against the corruption rife in the administration of the colonies and in Portugal itself.

Hipólito died in 1823, without knowing that he had been proclaimed consul of Brazil in England. He was buried in the Church of Saint Mary the Virgin, in Hurley, Berkshire, but in 2001 his remains were brought to Brazil, and can now be found at the Museu da Imprensa Nacional.

The three Masonic books Hipolito wrote, very rare today, were translated into Portuguese by Bro. João Nery Guimarães and will be published in the near future.

So with the seed of curiosity bearing the rich fruit of discovery, we find that the statue of the man seated on the throne known as Brother Hipólito José da Costa, was indeed the epitome of a Freemason. As a Mason, he was open-minded, intelligent, curious, and inquisitive. He was a man who was a free thinker in a time when narrow-minded ideas were the norm. He exhibited the additional ideals of toleration and compromise, the true attributes of a Freemason!

References & Acknowledgements

Carvalho, William – Hipólito da Costa, *Engenho & Arte* # 8, 2008

João Guilherme Ribeiro, Past Grand High Priest of Brazil, Masonic Author and Publisher

"Encyclopedia of Freemasonry", Albert G. Mackey 33°

PART II

Transactions 2023-2025

7

Historicity of the Arch and Keystone in Solomon's Temple

KEN JP STUCZYNSKI

{Presented 9 March 2023, Utica, NY at the Thomas Smith Webb Chapter of Research. Ken JP Stuczynski is a Past Master of Western New York Lodge of Research No.9007 and finishing his term as High Priest of Thomas Smith Web Chapter of Research No.1798 at the time of this publication.}

Author's Note: Much effort is spent attempting to validate myths and legends using the facts of history and science. This misleads us to believe their value is tied to conformity with outward truths. While we may be comforted by such validations, the author suggests this is neither necessary nor desirable. The purpose of this paper is not to dispel myth, but honor it. By piercing the veil of outward appearances, we pass to the eso-

teric. Such contradictions were likely intentional by the authors of ritual, and meant to amplify higher meaning, not detract from it.

Thesis

The arch and keystone are essential symbols of Royal Arch Masonry. We find them in ritual scenes of the First Temple in Jerusalem, Solomon's Temple, built in the 10th Century BCE. Did such an arch exist as historical fact? To answer this question, we will explore its plausibility based on the architecture of that time and place.

Introduction

An arch in its broadest sense is an entrance or support the sides of which slope toward each other at the top. Stone arches can be found in nearly all ancient civilizations, from Mesopotamia and the Mediterranean to India, China, and Meso-America. However, most of them are corbel or "false" arches, using overlapping stones that meet in the middle (Wikipedia 2020).

What we are looking for is a "true" arch, where voussoir (wedge-shaped stones) form a bow such that they all support each other in distributing weight. The keystone is laid last to make the arch-self-supporting and it may be larger or ornamental (Wikipedia 2022). Therefore, we will explore the appearance and use of true arches in ancient history and archaeology connected with Jewish culture during the time of the First Temple.

The Romans

The invention of the (true) Arch is commonly attributed to the Rome, who likely acquired it from Etruria and appeared at a similar time in Greece. The first example of a true arch, according to Levy, is the Etruscan Gate at Volterra, c. 4th Century BCE (Levy 2006, 8).

According to Durant, the History of Rome can be seen as the battle between the architrave (lintel) and the arch (Durant 1971, 339). The Roman aqueducts were built in the 4th BCE forward (National Geographic Society 2022). The Cloaca Maxima was enclosed in the 3rd century BC with a stone barrel vault (Britannica 2009). Architraves were replaced by arches in triumphal and decorative works circa 2nd C BC (Durant 1971, 92) and soon thereafter the "Arcate revolution" of Rome brought the arch to baths, theaters, circuses, stadiums, and theaters (Durant 1971, 359-360).

This is all fine, but Roman and even Etruscan culture does not predate the time in question. Therefore, we must look elsewhere.

The Greeks and Egyptians

The Greeks and Egyptians possessed the technology of arches, but generally didn't use it. Hanlon states that the "Egyptians and the Greeks understood the arch as a structural device and had the technological sophistication to use it to full advantage, yet they avoided it or relegated it to minor, inconsequential applications" (Hanlon 2006).

Regarding the Greeks, he described their use of arches and vaults "only in situations where the lateral thrust was easily counteracted by massive walls, as in fortifications, or by the earth in subterranean chambers" and that they were "highly conservative and examples before the Roman era are rare" (Hanlon 2006). Levy goes further, stating, "in Hellenistic architecture the arch was recognized as no more than a self-conscious tour de force" (Levy 2006, 8).

Regarding the Egyptians, Hanlon says they "appear to have had no interest in using the structural advantages of the arch above ground." He continues that By the beginning of the Third Dynasty (ca. 2686 BC), the Egyptians were masters of brick construction, including the use of arches and vaults. However, their only application of this technology was in burial chambers below ground, where brick was more durable than wood and where the lateral thrust of an arch or a vault was easily absorbed by the surrounding compacted earth (Hanlon 2006).

Durant concurs that the arch and vault in Egypt were used sparingly (Durant 1954, 185).

In this part of the paper, we should also consider the Myceneans, who were not only the predecessors of the Greeks, but were descended from Minoan civilization, which was also a progenitor of Phoenician culture. Hitchcock states that their building was "characterized by a liberal use of the corbel arch ... to build culverts in bridges, construct galleries and passageways, and create the domed beehive or tholos tombs". They distinctively used a relieving triangle to better distribute weight over an arch's lintel. Mycenean chamber tombs were carved out of rock rather than placing stone components (Hitchcock 2010). In other words, they did not use a true arch or vault.

The Semitic Peoples

Now we must look more closely at the origins of Semitic peoples, which trace back to Mesopotamia. The Sumerians were the first to use a true arch with a keystone, and did so in both private dwellings and the Royal Tombs at Ur (Barnouw 1971, 249).

Arched doors with voussoir were common at Ur in 2000 BCE (Durant 1954, 132).

However, due to the rarity of stone, almost all important Babylonian buildings were brick, and adobe was the common material for everything else. These later architectural designs were a "mass of straight lines", with only some arches and arched vaults mixed in (Durant 1954, 224-227).

The Semitic-speaking Assyrians, who used brick faced by stone, had arches and vaults, but still used beams for supporting roofs (Durant 1954, 181).

As an aside, as South Asia had contact with the Levant in ancient times, we should note that India didn't build in stone before the 3rd Century BCE (Durant 1954, 596).

From all this, we know true arches did exist in some, but not all, of the cultures that preceded those of Palestine. We know the arch was known in Egypt, from whence came Moses and the Twelve Tribes three centuries before Solomon and his Temple. However, they were sparsely used, or no longer used, by the 1st Millennium BCE.

Jewish (Phoenician) Architecture

Most directly pertinent is the architectural style of the Jewish people at the time of Solomon. We can recall that the Tribes of Israel were nomadic conquerors, not city-builders. Previous to the First Temple, even the Ark of the Covenant was kept in a tent surrounded by fences rather than a permanent structure. As such, there is no distinct ancient Jewish architecture. In "The Styles of Ornament", Speltz confirms this, saying, "The Hebrews in Palestine were entirely dependent on the Phoenicians for their technics [sic] and their art. ... The principal buildings of King Solomon's palace, and of the Temple were the work of Phoenician artists and artisans" (Speltz 1994, 34).

The problem is that little is known of Phoenician architecture, and the Jewish Temple is counted as one of its few examples. Except for foundations and harbors, they worked mostly in wood, a medium not commonly preserved in time. It is assumed wood architraves (lintels) were used in the Temple (Kendrick 1855, 250-251). Reconstructions of their buildings are conjecture (Rawlinson 1889, 250).

But did they use the arch? Most of what is left are tombs, and if not carved or of rock, tomb ceilings were either slabs or overlapping gables (Rawlinson 1889, 270). Quoting Renan's "Mission de Phénicie", Rawlinson states that "[n]othing conducts to the belief that the Phœnicians ever made use of the keyed vault" (Rawlinson 1889, 272). This paper's author was only able to find a simple relief in Assyrian Sennacherib that depicts a Phoenician city with a parabolic shape that may be a single arch of unknown style. All other openings are depicted as rectangular (Moscati 1968, 51).

What of religious edifices? The Phoenician King of Tyre erected temples in his city, but none remain (Rawlinson 1889, 253). However, according to Moscati, "The fullest information concerning [their] religious architecture is the biblical description of the [T]emple of Solomon".

Before we enter the inner sanctum of this paper by reviewing what is known of the Temple itself, we must consider one more ancient site. The Canaanite City Gate in Ashkelon is dated c.1850 BCE and "believed to be the most ancient arched gate in the world". A barrel-vaulted archway made of "calcareous sandstone (kurkar) and mud-bricks, the top of the arch collapsed in ancient times" (Madain Project 2023). Because the seaport had "alternating periods of construction and destruction" (Lefkovits 2008), and looking at the unusual stone pattern in photographs, this author considers suspect any assumption as to the original form of the arch (corbel or true).

The Temple Itself

There are two major sources describing the construction and design of the First Temple — scripture, namely 1 Kings (Chapters 5-8) and 2 Chronicles (Chapters 2-7), and the Jewish-Roman historian Flavius Josephus (b.37 CE) in his 8th Book of Antiquities. They describe only post and lintel construction, wooden doorframes, and no part of its dedication devoted to any architectural element. The account of Josephus also mentions that Solomon "had cut a doorway out of the wall". No arches were used as roof supports, as it was comprised of "very long beams" of timber (Josephus, Whiston, and Maier 1999, 272-273). In other words, neither the bible nor Josephus makes any mention of any arch or arches in construction or dedication.

Biblical descriptions of Solomon's Temple are also consistent with those of Syrian temples of the period, and show a dominant Egyptian influence (Moscati 1968, 44-45). Durant writes that its design was "in the style that the Phœnicians had adopted from Egypt, with decorative ideas from Assyria and Babylon" (Durant 1954, 307). The architecture of these cultures we have already covered.

And the design was simple, where the local people "forgivably looked upon it as one of the wonders of the world; they had not seen the immensely greater temples of Thebes, Babylon and Nineveh" (Durant 1954, 307).

Other Considerations

The Rabbinic writing, Mishnah Middot (c.190 – c.230 CE), describes the Second Temple's openings. "All the gates there had lintels except that of Taddi which had two stones inclined to one another" (Kulp 2023). This is not a true arch, or at least not one with a keystone, but resembles arches in 12th and 13th Century CE India by Qutub-ud-Din Aibak, who "cut the corbels in the shape of the true arch and put together a large array of arches that are really corbels impersonating the true arch. … [They] are all false arches" (Hashmi 2018). This informs us that even after the Jewish Exile, a true archway was not used in what we would expect to be an attempt to recreate the First Temple.

There is altogether a lack of other description sources of the First Temple as it was actually built. The longest of the Dead Sea Scrolls, the Temple Scroll, states that "Solomon should actually have built the First Temple as it is described here in the Temple Scroll", as it was written in the form of a revelation to Moses (Maier 1985, 59). Likewise, Ezekiel (40:1-42:20) recounts a vision during the exile, not a memory or witness to it. The Temple described in Enochian tradition is something else altogether – a heavenly Temple where G-d is enthroned (Nickelsburg 2013). As with other sources speaking of temples that should have been or might someday be, there is no reason to suppose a correlation in design worthy of consideration as evidence either way.

Conclusion

The details of the design of the First Temple in Jerusalem are sparse or unknown. But we do know there is no mention of any arch or arches in any authoritative text, and that the architectural culture of the builders and surrounding civilizations did not use true arches as a matter of course. The inclusion of any arch would be unique and different enough that there would have been mention of it. Therefore, it is not plausible that an arch with a keystone existed at that time and place. Ritual references to it are purely symbolic.

BIBLIOGRAPHY

Barnouw, Victor. "An Introduction to Anthropology". Homewood, Ill.: Dorsey Press, 1971.

Britannica, Editors of Encyclopaedia. "Cloaca Maxima | Ancient Structure, Rome, Italy." Encyclopedia Britannica, May 22, 2009. https://www.britannica.com/topic/Cloaca-Maxima.

Durant, Will [and Ariel]. "Caesar and Christ: A History of Roman Civilization and of Christianity from the Beginnings to A.D. 325". New York: MJF Books, 1971.

———. "Our Oriental Heritage : Being a History of Civilization in Egypt and the near East to the Death of Alexander, and in India, China and Japan from the Beginning to Our Own Day …" New York: Simon And Schuster, 1954.

Editors of the Madain Project. "Canaanite City Gate (Ashkelon) – Madain Project (En)." madainproject.com. Madain Project. Accessed February 16, 2023. https://madainproject.com/ashkelon_canaanite_city_gate.

Flavius Josephus, William Whiston, and Paul L Maier. "The New Complete Works of Josephus". Grand Rapids, Mi: Kregel Publications, 1999.

Hanlon, Don. "Arches and Culture." Nexus Network Journal 8, no. 2 (October 2006): 67–72. https://doi.org/10.1007/s00004-006-0018-6.

Hashmi, Sohail. "The Music of Stones: 700 Years of Adoption, Assimilation, Absorption and Appropriation." History for Peace. The Seagull Foundation for the Arts, August 5, 2018. https://www.historyforpeace.pw/post/the-music-of-stones-700-years-of-adoption-assimilation-absorption-and-appropriation.

Hitchcock, Louise A. "Mycenaean Architecture." In The Oxford Handbook of the Bronze Age Aegean (3000-1000 BCE), 200–209. Oxford: Oxford University Press, 2010. Kenrick, John. Phoenicia. London: B. Fellowes, 1855.

Kulp, Joshua. "Mishnah Middot 2:1." www.sefaria.org. Sefaria. Accessed February 13, 2023. https://www.sefaria.org/Mishnah_Middot.2.1.

Lefkovits, Etgar. "Oldest Arched Gate in the World Restored." The Jerusalem Post, April 8, 2008. https://www.jpost.com/local-israel/around-israel/oldest-arched-gate-in-the-world-restored.

Levy, Matthys. "The Arch: Born in the Sewer, Raised to the Heavens." Nexus Network Journal 8, no. 7-12 (2006). https://link.springer.com/content/pdf/10.1007/s00004-006-0014-x.pdf.

Madain Project, Editors. "Canaanite City Gate (Ashkelon)." madainproject.com. Encyclopedia of Abrahamic History & Archaeology. Accessed February 16, 2023. https://madainproject.com/ashkelon_canaanite_city_gate.

Maier, Johann. "The Temple Scroll: an Introduction, Translation & Commentary". Sheffield JSOT Press, 1985.

Moscati, Sabatino. "The World of the Phoenicians". New York: Praeger, 1968.

National Geographic Society. "Roman Aqueducts." education.nationalgeographic.org, May 20, 2022. https://education.nationalgeographic.org/resource/roman-aqueducts.

Nickelsburg, George W. E. "The Temple according to 1 Enoch." February 19, 2013. https://biblicalstudiesonline.wordpress.com/2016/01/18/george-w-e-nickelsburg-the-temple-according-to-1-enoch/.

Rawlinson, George. "The Story of Phoenicia". New York: Putnam's, 1889.

Speltz, Alexander. "Styles of Ornament". Gramercy, 1994.

Wikipedia Contributors. "Corbel Arch." Wikipedia. Wikimedia Foundation, August 25, 2020. https://en.wikipedia.org/wiki/Corbel_arch.

———. "Keystone (Architecture)." Wikipedia. Wikimedia Foundation, April 17, 2022. https://en.wikipedia.org/wiki/Keystone_(architecture).

APPENDIX

The following images portray the general structure of various arches {original image source unknown unless otherwise noted}:

(a) posts and lintel (also called "prop and lintel" or a trabeated system);

(b) columns (posts) with architrave only (lintel);

(c) corbel arch with small lintel stone in center {Wikipedia, user Ricraider};

(d) brick or stone corbel arch;

(e) corbel arch with stones faced to create a smooth curve {Wikipedia, user Anton};

(f) true arch, with many voussoirs but without a distinct keystone

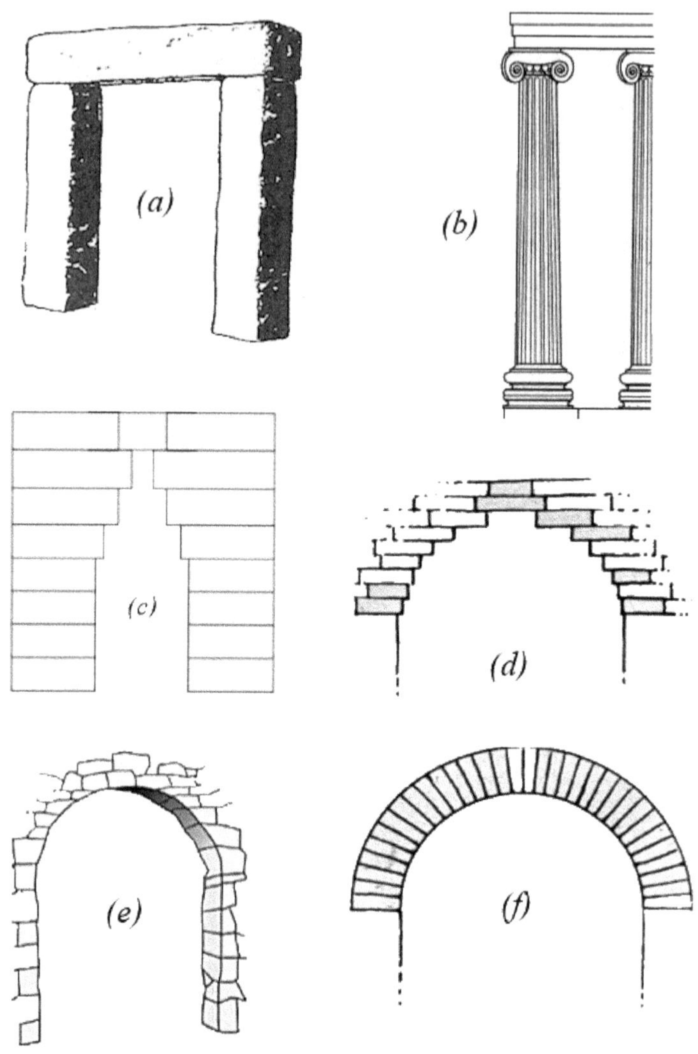
(a)
(b)
(c)
(d)
(e)
(f)

8

Halliwell Manuscript

CHRISTOPHER FOX

{Presented 24 June 2023 at Utica Masonic Temple.}

I was really taken in by the Regius poem or the Halliwell Manuscript as it was referred to after it was transcribed, which is the first and oldest documented text about Freemasonry, "It was written between 1350 and 1450 A.D. with the preponderance of authority dating it at about 1390"[1]. The Poem is still currently located in The British Library, where it has been rarely removed since being gifted by King George II, in 1757. George B.F. Kloss informs us that it is a copy of the book constitutions written by the general assembly held in the year 926 in the city of York. it was written about 1838-39, by Mr. James Orchard Halliwell (unfortunately, he was not a mason, but he did title it).

The manuscript itself is a rhymed verse poem, it is composed as a 794 lined 64 vellum paged middle English rhyming couplet. At the top of the poem is inscribed, "HIE incipuntconstituciones artis gemetriae secundum euclydem" or, "Here begins the Constitutions of the art of Geometry according to Euclid". This language proves it be older than the Wycliffe's Bible; which was the translation of the Bible by John Wycliffe an English Protestant into the common language in the early to mid-1300s; and in the previous paragraph, many already had a strong inkling of this anyway. Through the poem there is evidence that this was a Roman-Catholic production and was written when the religion of Rome prevailed in England, which always catches me off guard because I hear so much that in the past the Catholic church had said that you couldn't be a mason.

The first two verses hit my attentive ear extremely hard; not only because of the blatant words of geometry or mason but because they combined are one big prayer, and we always begin our important undertakings by first invoking the aid of deity and this lengthy work is no after supper crossword. The fourth verse talks about Euclid being from Egypt as well stating all men are equal. I felt this should be noted as all men are equal part that in the 1300s in Europe, slavery was still a social norm, but our fraternity still strove against it. In verse six everyone in the entire city pretty much becomes a Mason, including the leaders so in verse eight that is when fifteen articles and fifteen points will begin so that the men will be good, fair, and square leaders. The second article is a rule I've tried to keep vaulted in my faithful breast long before I knew this poem even existed but since I became a mason, and the eleventh; well, that has always been a personal preference of mine. The second states to attend lodge unless due to extreme illness or truly unable so that one may learn a valuable lesson; and the eleventh stresses not to work at night perhaps alluding to the 24-inch gauge lesson of whereby there are eight hours found for refreshment and sleep. I took from the fifth, seventh, and fifteenth as ways of protecting the craft; in a small way from cowans but mainly by keeping it strong and steadfast. The cowans came from article seven, where "That no master for favor nor dread shall no thief neither cloth nor feed, thieves he shall harbor never one." This goes the same with murderers as well; so, neither should you even associate with these individuals in your daily lives but don't ever think about bringing them to the craft. When it comes to keeping the Craft strong and steadfast, the fifth and fifteenth and last article, I feel are the best at that; the fifth states let none that are lame and only have all their limbs. Today the lame would be permissible, but the limbs would be excusable, but I believe back then if you couldn't easily multi-task difficult things working and bringing home enough to eat let alone enough for dues would be almost impossible. And the final article breaks down mainly to be true to one another. As I could go on and on about this work of art I will have to summarize the rest; the points describe how to be a good leader and master to an apprentice and after that it goes on to explain how a mason should act outside of the lodge This manuscript has also been taken to been being called the, " Legend of the Craft" Beyond the bare story it contains, discover some key to the true origin and nature upon which our fraternity and brotherhood took root and grew from. The following are the 15 Articles written:

> Article 1. A master mason must be worthy of the confidence of the lords; he must pay the fellows a fair wage with the lord's money.
> Article 2. Every master mason must attend a general assembly, unless he can give a good excuse.

> Article 3. A master mason shall not take on an apprentice for less than seven years and must lodge him during his apprenticeship.
> Article 4. A master mason must not take any serfs as apprentice.
> Article 5. A master mason shall take on neither bastards nor cripples.
> Article 6. A apprentice shall be paid less than the fellows, but his salary shall increase as he progresses.
> Article 7. A master mason shall employ neither thieves nor murderers.
> Article 8. A master mason may discharge an incompetent worker and replace him with another.
> Article 9. A master mason must make sure that the foundation of the building is well-laid.
> Article 10. A master mason must never take over, or meddle with, the work of another master mason, or be fined a penalty of ten pounds.
> Article 11. A mason shall not work at night, except to study.
> Article 12. One shall not disparage the work of one's fellows.
> Article 13. A master mason must give his apprentice a complete education.
> Article 14. A master mason shall not take on an apprentice unless he has enough work for him.
> Article 15. A master mason must not leave his fellows astray, because he must care about their souls.[2]

After reading the articles out loud, a thought about the 14th stanza arose. A common cry we make within our lodges is, "we need more members"; but the question is, is that really what we need? Many Brethren have left our sacred halls in the past because of disinterest and boredom, whether it is because of the over used phrase, "back in my day..." or many lodges merely opening, doing business, and then closing without even fellowship after. Do we truly have "enough work"? Or, in some cases we push these newer Brethren to feats they are not ready for, such as in the 3rd , 9th, and 13th stanza, some masons have become presiding officers of lodges in less than five years of joining and that has scared Brethren to leave as well. What modifications to our actions in the lodges can be made to raise the "work" newer masons can accomplish to make them feel apart and of use to the Fraternity; and how, not only their top line signers but the lodge as a whole can be both mentor and assessors of the foundation for them. The thought that struck me was, as we model ourselves to be that of a perfect ashlar; the hewn parts of our old selves, our "rough" selves should be examined and utilized as steppingstones for the future. This is so that they too can advance confidently in their journey.

CITATIONS

[1] Peter, David M. *The Regius Manuscript*. Last modified November 6, 2012. http://mastermason.com/davidmpeter/research/regius.htm#:~:text=The%20Regius%20Manuscript%20is%20one%20of%20the%20oldest,preponderance%20of%20authority%20dating%20it%20at%20about%201390. 1 Peter, David M. The Regius Manuscript. Last modified November 6, 2012.

[2] Donohugh, Shawn. Los Angeles Harbor Lodge. https://www.sanpedromasons.org/2017/11/regius-manuscript

9

The Three Signs of the Veils

MICHAEL D. WEISBERG

{Presented 24 June 2023 at Utica Masonic Temple. Michael D. Weisberg is a Past High Priest of Latham Chapter No.168, and a Grand Chaplain for the Grand Lodge of the State of New York at the time of this printing.}

There is a piece of the Royal Arch ritual that we hear at each meeting that is easy to overlook but teaches a significant lesson about how we should approach our personal faith. These are the three signs of the masters of the veils. To wit:

1. An imitation of that given by the Lord unto Moses when he commanded him to cast his rod upon the ground,
2. An imitation of that given by the Lord unto Moses

when he commanded him to put his hand into his bosom, and

3. An imitation of that given by the Lord unto Moses when he commanded him to pour water upon the dry land.

These are potent symbols, but how should we view them, and what do they mean? Let's start with the first. In Exodus 4:1–5:

> And Moses answered and said: 'But, behold, they will not believe me, nor hearken unto my voice; for they will say: The lord hath not appeared unto thee.' And the LORD said unto him: 'What is that in thy hand?' And he said: 'A rod.' And He said: 'Cast it on the ground.' And he cast it on the ground, and it became a serpent; and Moses fled from before it. And the LORD said unto Moses: 'Put forth thy hand, and take it by the tail—and he put forth his hand, and laid hold of it, and it became a rod in his hand—that they may believe that the LORD, the God of their fathers, the God of Abraham, the God of Isaac, and the God of Jacob, hath appeared unto thee.'

This simple transformation was used to show Moses, who had lost faith that he was the chosen of the Lord, that the Lord's power could move him. It showed him that, despite his doubt, that the Lord was with him.

In Exodus 4:6–8, the Lord further illustrated that his wonder was beyond the comprehension of the Pharaoh and his court.

> And the LORD said furthermore unto him: 'Put now thy hand into thy bosom.' And he put his hand into his bosom; and when he took it out, behold, his hand was leprous, as white as snow. And He said: 'Put thy hand back into thy bosom.—And he put his hand back into his bosom; and when he took it out of his bosom, behold, it was turned again as his other flesh.— And it shall come to pass, if they

> will not believe thee, neither hearken to the voice of the first sign, that they will believe the voice of the latter sign.

In ancient times, the one most feared disease was Leprosy. There was no cure, it was debilitating, it carried a deep social stigma, and was always fatal. In this simple sign, the Lord demonstrated that he was both able to curse and to cure. It was an example of an impossible act performed by the Lord, who is omnipotent.

Finally, the Lord foretells his support of the children of Israel when he says to Moses in Exodus 4:9:

> And it shall come to pass, if they will not believe even these two signs, neither hearken unto thy voice, that thou shalt take of the water of the river, and pour it upon the dry land; and the water which thou takest out of the river shall become blood upon the dry land.'

This created a causal relationship between the lack of faith of the Pharaoh and the plagues that were visited upon Egypt.

It is these signs that are chosen by the Royal Arch to be the signs of the Masters of the Veils. They illustrate in the most direct manner the faith we place in the Lord at times of need and how that faith is strengthened and assured by the actions of the Lord.

Interestingly, the next verses reflect Moses's lack of faith in his own abilities and how the Lord accommodated his needs by sending Aaron with him to the Pharaoh. Thus, demonstrating both the Lord's might and His compassion.

There is also significant foreshadowing in these verses. We again see the casting of the rod upon the ground when Moses demonstrates the might of the Lord before the pharaoh and his magicians. In this case, Moses is both full in his faith, and when the magicians attempt to duplicate what is done, the staff of Moses devours the false transformations of the magicians.

The lesson of G-d's power to save from death foreshadows the death of the first-born of Egypt, when he warns the Children of Israel to paint the doorposts of their houses with lamb's blood to prevent the deaths in their households. Another demonstration of the purview of G-D over life and death.

The pouring of the water is doubly foreshadowing. It does foreshadow the first plague, but it also foreshadows Moses' downfall. In failing to strictly obey the command of G-D, Moses strikes the rock to make water flow, rather than simply raising his staff. This failing of faith results in his being unable to enter the promised land.

We, as Royal Arch Masons, should heed the lesson contained herein. Our faith should be unswerving, our willingness to carry the message unerring, and our ability to see the work done bound up with our very being. This is our Fervency and Zeal!

From the verses that follow, we also learn that we can reach our ends through mercy, kindness, and compassion. Leaving none behind because of simple disability or personal inadequacy.

Let all of us carefully consider this the next time someone stumbles in their ritual, their personal business, or their lives. These are the signs presented to us in the Great Light!

So, these are our signs as Royal Arch Masons!

10

The Prophet Haggai

JEFFREY M. WILLIAMSON AND DONALD WILLIAMS

{Presented at the Joint Meeting of the Thomas Smith Webb Chapter of Research No. 1798, Ohio Chapter of Research, and Western New York Lodge of Research, on October 13, 2023, at the Temple in Lackawanna, New York. Don Williams is a member of Tonawanda Keystone Chapter No.71.}

It is interesting to note that every major concordant body of Freemasonry references or chronicles the destruction of Jerusalem and the sacking of the Temple by the Chaldeans in the year 586 B.C.

Historically, we discover that under the direction of King Nebuchadnezzar, the Hebrew nation was defeated; its citizens were taken into captivity, and the plundered spoils of war, consisting of the Jewish treasures, Sacred Vessels, and Holy Furniture of the Temple, were carried off to Babylon.

As a climax to this saga, we learn of the eventual freedom of the exiles, and the efforts of Zerubbabel, a Prince of the House of Judah, along with his band of companions who successfully rebuilt the Temple in Jerusalem in 516 B.C.

Against this historical backdrop the ceremonies, rituals and lessons of the Royal Arch Chapter, the Cryptic Council, the Chivalric Order of the Red Cross, the Knight Masons of the U.S.A, and the 15th & 16th Degrees of the Princes of Jerusalem of the Scottish Rite, (just to name a few!) are portrayed at length and transmitted to candidates who seek additional enlightenment in our venerable Order.

The infrastructure and platform of Royal Arch Masonry is set in the ruins of the first Temple, with Jeshua (Ezra 3:2) (or Joshua), Zerubbabel, and Haggai taking major portions as the principal characters of this noteworthy period. Our Royal Arch tradition, fancies these individuals comprising the first Grand Council, however I cannot locate any Scriptural or written accounts to base this assertion.

The purpose of this discourse is to add to our base of knowledge concerning the Prophet Haggai. He is one of the principal characters named in the above construct. It is intriguing to contemplate why the designers of our ritual deemed Haggai reasonably important to include him in our ceremonies.

It is without dispute that Haggai's name is pronounced at the ritualistic opening ceremony of every Convocation, but few Companions (if any) are fluent in the history and background concerning this oracle. Who is Haggai? What is his role during this era? How did he accomplish his task?

In pursuing our objective, we will attempt to interpret and explore the scriptural passages of the Book of Haggai contained in the Old Testament of the Holy Bible. Through this analysis, we hope to gain knowledge concerning the events and the society of his era, thus providing an even deeper appreciation and understanding of this important Masonic setting.

The Book of Haggai is named after the Prophet Haggai, whose name means "festive" or "festival." Many believe the name was given because Haggai was born on or near a festival day. It is also the second shortest book in the Old Testament.

Haggai is also the most precisely dated book of the Bible, with the dates of each sermon given to the exact day. The accuracy with which he records these dates suggests that he might have kept a journal. The beginning of Darius' reign is well established at 522 B.C. Each of his four messages took place in the second year of his reign, which would be 520 B.C.

His writings also suggest that he had seen the glory of King Solomon's Temple, which would make him at least 70 years of age when he wrote his prophecy. Haggai most likely returned to Jerusalem from Babylon with Zerubbabel 18 years earlier, in 538 B.C.

As a result of the proclamation of King Cyrus, Israel was allowed to return from Babylon to her homeland under the civil leadership of Zerubbabel and the spiritual guidance of Joshua the High Priest. About 50,000 Jews returned. In 536 B.C., they began to rebuild the Temple, but opposition from the neighbors and indifference by the returning Jews, caused the work to be abandoned.

Sixteen years later, Haggai was commissioned by the Lord to stir up the people not only to rebuild the Temple, but also to reorganize their "spiritual priorities". As a result, the Temple was completed four years later. (516 B.C.)

The primary theme is the rebuilding of God's Temple, which had been lying in ruins since its destruction in 586 B.C. By means of five messages from the Lord, Haggai exhorted the people to renew their efforts to build the house of the Lord. He motivated them by noting that the drought and crop failures were caused by misplaced spiritual priorities.

But to Haggai, the rebuilding of the Temple was not an end in itself. The Temple represented God's dwelling place, His presence with His chosen people. The destruction of the Temple by the Chaldeans followed the departure of God's dwelling glory.

To the Prophet Haggai, the rebuilding of the Temple invited the return of God's presence to their midst. Using the historical situation as a springboard, Haggai puts across the idea of the glorious messianic temple yet to come and encourages them with the promise of even greater peace, prosperity, divine sovereignty, and national blessing during the millennium.

I invite you to follow along with our review of "The Book of Haggai". We will incorporate appropriate commentary and interpretations as necessary as we look forward to obtaining the answers to the queries previously put forward.

The Book of Haggai, Chapter 1

*1 In the second year of King Darius, in the sixth month, on the first day of the month, the word of the Lord came by Haggai the prophet to Zerubbabel the son of Shealtiel, governor of Judah, and to Joshua the son of Jehozadak, the high priest, saying, 2 "Thus speaks the Lord of hosts, saying: '***This people says,*** *"The time has not come, the time that the Lord's house should be built."*

Verse 1: King Darius 1 became King of Persia in 521 B.C. and ascended to the throne after the death of Cambyses. He was an officer of Cambyses and the great-grandson of Cyrus the Great's brother. He reigned until his death in 486 B.C.

Zerubbabel was the grandson of Jehoiachin and thus was in the Davidic line. He was the civil leader and overseer of the Temple rebuilding project. He re-established the Davidic throne, even though it would not be occupied again until the time of the Messiah.

Joshua (also spelled "Jeshua" in other writings) was the High Priest and a descendant of Zadok and the religious leader of the exiled community that returned to Jerusalem. He re-established the High Priest line of Aaron through Eleazar. Jehozadak was one of Nebuchadnezzar's captives.

Verse 2: Haggai begins his message by quoting the popular point of view of the people, saying that it was not yet time to rebuild the Temple. These sentiments were fueled by the hostile opposition of their neighbors and the lack of economic prosperity in the region. The roots of their reluctance ultimately lay in their selfish indifference to the Lord.

God's displeasure and distance is noted in His reference to them as "This people" and not "My People." They wanted wealth for themselves, not a Temple!

> **3** Then the word of the Lord came by Haggai the prophet, saying,
> 4 "Is it time for you yourselves to dwell in your paneled houses, and
> **this temple to lie in ruins**?"

Verse 4: Speaks of the people's self-indulgence. The Prophet's rhetorical question demonstrated their hypocrisy and misplaced priorities. Walls and ceilings overlaid with cedar were common in wealthy residences and had to be imported from Lebanon at great expense.

> **5** Now therefore, thus says the Lord of hosts: "Consider your ways!
> **6** "You have sown much, and bring in little; You eat, but do not have
> enough; You drink, but you are not filled with drink; You clothe
> yourselves, but no one is warm; And he who earns wages, Earns
> wages to put into a bag with holes." 7 Thus says the Lord of hosts:
> "Consider your ways!

Verse 6: By using five pairs of poetic contrasts, each question results in the same conclusion. Haggai paints a vivid picture of their economic and social distress. Their selfish lack of concern for God's house had only cost them more hardship.

With a biting query, the Lord reminded them that it was not right for them to live in expensive paneled houses while the Temple lay in ruins and urged them to carefully consider the consequences of their indifference.

> **8** Go up to the mountains and bring wood and build the temple, that
> I may take pleasure in it and be glorified," says the Lord.

Verse 8: Three imperatives give the remedy for their trouble — *Go up! Bring wood! Build!* The long captivity of 70 years had let the forest grow so there was an ample supply of wood. They were to use it to rebuild the House of the Lord, and therein He would be glorified.

By putting God first, He would then be honored in their worship, and they would be blessed in the secondary matters of life.

> **9** "You looked for much, but indeed it came to little; and when you
> brought it home, I blew it away. Why?" says the Lord of hosts.

> "Because of My house that is in ruins, while every one of you runs to his own house.

Verse 9: The people ran to their own house, because they were zealous to pursue their own interest, the prophet drew a contrast between the one who eagerly ran to care for "his own house" while disregarding God's house.

> **10** Therefore the heavens above you withhold the dew, and the earth withholds its fruit. 11 For I called for a drought on the land and the mountains, on the grain and the new wine and the oil, on whatever the ground brings forth, on men and livestock, and on all the labor of your hands."

Verse 10, 11: An economic catastrophe resulted from God's withholding of the summer dew. That was the price for their disobedience. Grain, wine, and oil were the primary crops of the land. Cattle also languished because of the absence of spiritual health.

> **12** Then Zerubbabel the son of Shealtiel, and Joshua the son of Jehozadak, the high priest, with all the remnant of the people, **obeyed** the voice of the Lord their God, and the words of Haggai the prophet, as the Lord their God had sent him; and the people **feared** the presence of the Lord. **13** Then Haggai, the Lord's messenger, spoke the Lord's message to the people, saying, "**I am with you**, says the Lord."

Verse 12-15: Haggai's second message came twenty-three days after the first one, around September 21, 520 B.C. The Lord's call to "Consider your ways" caused the people to respond in repentance and obedience.

Verse 13: This new message of "*I am with you*" further stirred the Jews to action. Oppressed by hostilities from without and famine from within, the Lord responded to their genuine repentance and obedience, assuring them of His presence with them.

> **14** So the Lord stirred up the spirit of Zerubbabel the son of Shealtiel, governor of Judah, and the spirit of Joshua the son of Jehozadak, the high priest,

Verse 14: The Lord energized the leaders and the people through his Word to carry on the work of rebuilding the Temple. Just as God had moved in the heart of Cyrus 16 years earlier, the people's response of repentance and obedience allowed God's Spirit to energize them for the task.

> and the spirit of **all the remnant** of the people:

Verse 14: Refers to the exiles who returned from Babylon and took the message to heart. Realizing that the words of the prophet were from the Lord, they "obeyed" and "feared" knowing that God was present.

> and they came and worked on the house of the Lord of hosts, their God, **15** on the twenty-fourth day of the sixth month, in the second year of King Darius.

Haggai Chapter 2

> **1** In the seventh month, on the twenty-first of the month, the word of the Lord came by Haggai the prophet, saying:

Verse 1: This day in the month of Tishri corresponds to October 17, 520 B.C. This was the final day of the Feast of the Tabernacles. This feast celebrated God's provision for Israel during her 40 years of wandering in the wilderness. It gives thanks for a bountiful harvest. On this occasion, the Lord gave Haggai the third message.

> 2 "Speak now to Zerubbabel the son of Shealtiel, governor of Judah, and to Joshua the son of Jehozadak, the high priest, and to the remnant of the people, saying:

Verse 2: The first message was directed to the leaders, Zerubbabel, and Joshua. Here the prophet includes the remainder of the exiles who returned from Babylon.

> 3 'Who is left among **you who saw** this temple in its former glory? And how do you see it now? In comparison with it, is this not in your eyes as nothing?

Verse 3: Some of the people including Haggai had seen the magnificent Temple of Solomon before its destruction. With three figurative questions, the Lord through Haggai draws attention to the fact that this Temple was inferior to Solomon's Temple which caused many to be dispirited by its lack of splendor.

> 4 Yet now be strong, Zerubbabel,' says the Lord; 'and be **strong**, Joshua, son of Jehozadak, the high priest; and be strong, all you people of the land,' says the Lord, 'and **work**; for **I am with you**,' says the Lord of hosts.

Verse 4: To counteract the disenchantment the Lord repeated the command to "be strong" and to "work" assuring them of God's presence. This was the second reminder from the Lord "I am with you".

> 5 According to the word that I covenanted with you **when you came out of Egypt**, so My Spirit remains among you; do not fear!'

Verse 5: Spoken at the close of the feast commemorating God's provision during the wandering in the wilderness, His covenant commitment and promise that His Spirit would be with them as "when you came out of Egypt" would be most reassuring.

> 6 "For thus says the Lord of hosts: 'Once more (it is a little while) I will shake heaven and earth, the sea and dry land; 7 and **I will shake all nations**, and they shall come to the **Desire of All Nations**, and **I will fill this temple with glory**,' says the Lord of hosts.

Verse 6-7: The shaking of the cosmic bodies and the nations goes far beyond the historical removal of kingdoms and the establishment of others, such as the defeat of Persia by Greece. Rather, the text looks into the cataclysm in the universe described in Rev: 6-19, the subjugation of the nations by the Messiah, and the setting up of His kingdom, which will never be destroyed.

Verse 7: *the desire of all nations* is a reference to the Messiah, the Deliverer for whom all the nations ultimately long.

Verse 7: *I will fill this Temple with glory.* There is no Scripture to indicate that God's Glory ever did come to Zerubbabel's Temple. According to the Babylonian Talmud, the Temple of Zerubbabel was quite comparable to the Temple of Solomon except for five items that it did not have: (1) The Ark of the Covenant; (2) The Sacred Fire; (3) The Shekinah; (4) The Holy Spirit; and (5) The Urim and Thummim. This would indicate that the House itself was not greatly inferior to the one it supplanted.

> 8 'The silver is Mine, and the gold is Mine,' says the Lord of hosts.

Verse 8: Economically destitute, the people were reassured that He is the possessor of all things.

> 9 The glory of **this latter temple** shall be greater than the former,' says the Lord of hosts. 'And in this place **I will give peace**,' says the Lord of hosts."

Verse 1-9: With building operations in full swing, the Lord gave a strong message of encouragement, especially to the elderly among them who had seen Solomon's Temple. The Lord urged the people to be courageous, assuring them of his presence. His faithfulness to His covenant promises a greater, more glorious Temple in the future.

Verse 9: this latter temple...The Jews viewed the Temple in Jerusalem as one Temple existing in different forms at different times. The rebuilt Temple was considered a continuation of Solomon's Temple. However, the glory of the millennial Temple, the latter Temple will far surpass even the grandeur of Solomon's Temple. (The former Temple)

Verse 9: I will give thee peace...This peace is not limited to that peace which He gives to believers, but looks ahead to that ultimate peace when He returns to rule as the Prince of Peace upon the Throne of David in Jerusalem.

> **10** On the twenty-fourth day of the ninth month, in the second year of Darius, the word of the Lord came by Haggai the prophet, saying,

Verse 10-19: The fourth message of Haggai occurred 2 months after the third on the 24th day of the month of Chislev, corresponding to December 18, 520 B.C. This message sought to demonstrate that while their disobedience caused God's Blessings to be withheld, their obedience would reward them with His blessings.

> **11** "Thus says the Lord of hosts: 'Now, ask the priests concerning the
> law, saying, **12** If one carries holy meat in the fold of his garment,
> and with the edge he touches bread or stew, wine or oil, or any food,
> will it become holy?" ' " Then the priests answered and said, "No."
> **13** And Haggai said, "If one who is unclean because of a dead body

> touches any of these, will it be unclean?" So the priests answered and said, "It shall be unclean." **14** Then Haggai answered and said, " 'So is this people, and so is this nation before Me,' says the Lord, 'and so is every work of their hands; and what they offer there is unclean.

Verse 11-14: This passage provides an analogy or object lesson for the people; two questions were asked of the priests relative to ceremonial law. The first question was intended to show that ceremonial cleanliness cannot be transferred. Haggai then applies the lesson. Even though the people had been bringing their offerings while neglecting the rebuilding of the Temple, their offerings had not been acceptable. Their sin had caused their sacrifices to be contaminated and ineffectual. And their good works, their offerings, could not transmit cleanliness. In other words, sin is contagious, righteousness is not!

> **15** 'And now, carefully consider from this day forward: from before stone was laid upon stone in the temple of the Lord — **16** since those days, when one came to a heap of twenty ephahs, there were but ten; when one came to the wine vat to draw out fifty baths from the press, there were but twenty.

Verse 16: Ephahs and baths convert to four to six gallons, respectively.

> **17** I struck you with blight and mildew and hail in all the labors of your hands; yet you did not turn to Me,' says the Lord.

Verse 15-18: The Lord called the people to again consider their situation prior to the resumption of the Temple building. In those days, the farmer found less than expected. Between 50 to 60 percent of the expected harvest had been lost.

> **18** `Consider now from this day forward, from the twenty-fourth

> day of the ninth month, from the day that the foundation of the Lord's temple was laid–consider it:
> **19** Is the seed still in the barn? As yet the vine, the fig tree, the pomegranate, and the olive tree have not yielded fruit. But from this day I will bless you.' "
> **20** And again the word of the Lord came to Haggai on the twenty-fourth day of the month, saying,
> **21** "Speak to Zerubbabel, governor of Judah, saying: 'I will shake heaven and earth.
> **22** I will overthrow the throne of kingdoms; I will destroy the strength of the Gentile kingdoms. I will overthrow the chariots And those who ride in them; The horses and their riders shall come down, Every one by the sword of his brother.
> **23** '**In that day**,' says the Lord of hosts, 'I will take you, Zerubbabel My servant, the son of Shealtiel,' says the Lord,

Verse 23: Refers to the day of the Messiah's triumph, "My servant" is a distinctly Davidic and messianic title,

> 'and will make you like a signet ring; for I have chosen you,' says the Lord of hosts."

Verse 23: The signet ring was a symbol of honor, authority, and power. It corresponded to a king's scepter, which was used to seal letters and decrees. Zerubbabel, as God's signet ring, stands as the official representative of the Davidic dynasty and represents the resumption of the messianic line interrupted by the Exile.

Just as Pharaoh gave Joseph his signet ring and made him second in the kingdom, so God will do for the Davidic line of kings, the pre-Exilic signet of Jehoiachin was removed by God and renewed here by his grandson, Zerubbabel, who reestablished the Davidic line of Kings which would culminate in the millennium reign of Christ.

Zerubbabel appears in the line of Christ on both Joseph's side and Mary's side, thus bypassing God's curse on the lines of Jehoiakim and Jehoiachin.

Verse 20-23: The fifth message to Zerubbabel came on the same day as the fourth, and He returned to the theme of the millennial reign of the Messiah. Once again, it depicted the overthrow of the kingdom of the world and the establishment of the messianic kingdom. As the events predicted did not transpire historically, the promise pertains to the royal line through which the Messiah would come. It looked to the ultimate day when the Messiah reigns on the earth.

Summary and Conclusion

Although the biblical scholars categorize Haggai a minor prophet, we, as Royal Arch Masons and claimants to the title of "Sons of Light," can draw many life lessons from his divinely inspired words. His principles are as relevant in today's society as they were during his age.

1. Haggai admonished the people for having misplaced their priorities. He pointed out the errors of their ways, chasing after the luxuries of life while ignoring God's plan.
2. The people responded to God's message by resuming the work on the Temple. Their newfound obedience reconciled them back to God.
3. The people's courage and motivation came from the promise of God's presence and His peace. This is the peace of mind that comes from knowing that God is in control.

4. Haggai also dealt with the issues of living clean and godly lives so they would not defile their work and sacrifices. He also urged them to depend on God for life.
5. And finally, Haggai ultimately gave them hope for the future by revealing that God was going to destroy their enemies and establish His kingdom for His chosen people.

Haggai's exertions ultimately resulted in a series of events that led to the completion of the rebuilding of the Temple. Its completion was a momentous occasion for it marked the start of a new religious life for the Jewish people. The common people were given an understanding of the Law of Jehovah, and this led to a more spiritual concept of religion. Without the Temple, the Jewish faith could not possibly have blossomed forth into the mature and beneficent religion we recognize today.

As one of the principal characters of the Royal Arch Masonry ritual, the Prophet Haggai is, beyond a doubt, worthy of our admiration and respect. His role was substantial, and he accomplished the task God set before him. He is a true role model for all Royal Arch Companions.

REFERENCES AND RESOURCE MATERIALS FOR THIS PAPER

"New King James Bible"

"The Temples in Jerusalem" by Eversull

"The MacArthur Study Bible" by MacArthur

"The Old Past Master's Masonic Almanac" 6004 A.L., by M.·.E.·. Jan L. Beaderstadt, KYCH

11

Masons Associated with the Early Years of Ohio University

JEFF SLATTERY

{Originally Prepared for Ohio Lodge of Research, given on May 15, 2010. Presented at the Joint Meeting of the Thomas Smith Webb Chapter of Research No. 1798, Ohio Chapter of Research, and Western New York Lodge of Research, on October 13, 2023, at the Temple in Lackawanna, New York. S. Jefferson Slattery, KYCH, is a Past Master of Paramuthia Lodge No.25. He was serving as High Priest of Ohio Chapter of Research at the time of this presentation.}

Ohio University, located in Athens, Ohio, is the oldest university in Ohio and was the first institution of higher learning in the Northwest Territory. It is also the ninth-oldest public university in the United States. Many Masons were among the founders, early students, and faculty of Ohio University.

The Ohio Company of Associates or Ohio Company (not to be confused with the Ohio Company of Virginia) was the first non-American Indian group to settle in present-day Ohio. It was founded March 1, 1786, by Rufus Putnam, Benjamin Tupper, Samuel Holden Parsons, and Manasseh Cutler. In a meeting at the Bunch of Grapes Tavern in Boston, Massachusetts, they made plans for establishing settlements in Marietta, Chillicothe, and Athens under terms established in the Northwest Ordinance. The Ohio Company had purchased 1,500,000 acres of land north of the Ohio River and east of the Scioto River. They had planned to purchase more land to the west but that had been purchased by the Scioto Company.

Athens was originally known as Middletown because it was halfway between Marietta and Chillicothe. Athens was intended to be the home of an institution of democratic and open higher education, what would become known as Ohio University. Ohio University was chartered in 1804, one year after Ohio became a state. Manasseh Cutler, a close friend of George Washington and Thomas Jefferson, would be one of the main founders of Ohio University. The oldest building on campus, which contains the offices of the president, is called Cutler Hall in his honor.

The first settlement established by the Ohio Company was at Marietta, where the first military lodge under the Grand Lodge of Massachusetts met and eventually became the present American Union Lodge #1 under the Grand Lodge of Ohio. As we know from Ohio Masonic history, Rufus Putnam, one of the original members of American Union #1 would become our first Grand Master in 1808. Putnam presided over the first meeting of the

Ohio Company and was overseer of much of the survey work for the Ohio Company lands, including Athens and Ohio University. Putnam Hall, which is named for him, originally housed the elementary school that was used for the training of teachers (it is located next to McCracken Hall, which houses the College of Education). For many years, the Ohio University childcare center occupied the building which is now used by the School of Dance. Putnam was a member of the first board of trustees of Ohio University.

Putnam would become a Supreme Court judge for the Northwest Territory and was later appointed by President George Washington as the first Surveyor General of the United States. He is buried in Mound Cemetery in Marietta, where the Grand Lodge of Ohio erected and dedicated a long overdue monument to him on July 4, 2008, the year of the 200th anniversary of the Grand Lodge.

General Benjamin Tupper was born in 1738. He was a tanner as a young man and later taught school. When the Revolutionary War began, he entered as a lieutenant. He would later serve as lieutenant colonel, colonel, and left the army with the rank of brigadier general. He also served as a Supreme Court judge for the Northwest Territory. He was another of the original members of American Union #1 and had served as Master. The first campus building named for him was erected in 1883. There have been several in different locations over the years. The present building bearing his name is located on the east part of the College Green across from Memorial Auditorium. It was formerly known as the "Ag" building and also housed the Department of Home Economics. The building is now closed. Due to the age of the building, the university is considering whether to renovate, replace, or remove it. (Note: Tupper Hall is still standing and offers office and academic space, while other buildings are renovated)

In 1797, those who would establish the settlement at Athens made their way in boats down the Ohio River from Marietta to the mouth of the Hockhocking River and thence upstream to previously surveyed townships 8 and 9, which would become known as Alexander and Athens townships, respectively. In that first group of settlers were Silas Bingham, his brother Alvin, Edmund Williams, Barak Dorr, Isaac Barker, William Harper, John Wilkins, Robert Linzee, John Chandler and Johnathan Walker. The Bingham brothers and Isaac Barker were three of the first members of Paramuthia Lodge #25, which was chartered in January 1814.

Jacob Lindly (also seen spelled as Lindley as in the campus building named in his honor) was originally from Washington County, Pennsylvania. He was educated at Jefferson College and Princeton University. After coming to Ohio, he was a minister in Waterford near Marietta and later came to Athens, where he started the First Presbyterian Church. He became the first president of Ohio University and was a member of Paramuthia Lodge #25. Lindly would become Treasurer of Paramuthia in 1815. He was elected (or appointed?) Grand Chaplain of the Grand Lodge of Ohio in 1816. He remained as president of the university until 1822 and as an instructor in Mathematics and Rhetoric and Moral Philosophy until 1828, when he moved to Cincinnati to pursue his ministerial work. The university would confer an honorary Doctor of Divinity degree upon him in 1853. His pulpit chair is still used by the university at commencement and other highly ceremonial occasions. He died in 1857.

Lindly oversaw construction of the first building of the university, a 24-by-40-foot, two-room structure which was erected in 1808 behind the present Memorial Auditorium, where Galbreath Chapel now stands. Some later students would live in this building. Other students took up residence with village residents.

The first three students who were not quite ready for college-level education were educated in the community at the academy level and would eventually enter the university. They were Joel Abbot, John Perkins, and Brewster Higgins. All would eventually join Paramuthia Lodge.

One of the first instructors recruited by Jacob Lindly was Calvary Morris. Morris did not have a degree himself, but became very informed through his own study. Lindly would direct Morris on what to study so he could stay ahead of his students. He taught for Lindly at the university for two years, later becoming a university trustee. As trustee, Morris pushed for the closing off of the college green, which had served multiple community functions as a parade ground, market area, and a place for local residents' sheep to graze. Morris would eventually join and become very active in Paramuthia Lodge. He served as Junior Warden in 1822 and 1823, then as Master and representative to Grand Lodge in 1824. Morris was a leader in the local Methodist Episcopal church congregation.

Morris also served in a variety of public offices. He served as sheriff for four years, five terms in the Ohio General Assembly, three terms as a member of Congress and two terms as a probate judge. While in Congress, he supported the construction of the Hocking Canal. He left public service in 1843 to raise sheep and eventually left the area in 1847.

A follow-up history of the Masons from the mid-1800's is being developed.

References:

Answers.com. Ohio University. Retrieved May 7, 2010, from http://www.answers.com/topic/ohio-university

National Park Service. Rufus Putnam. Retrieved April 30, 2010, fromhttp://www.nps.gov/history/museum/exhibits/revwar/image_gal/indeimg/putnam.html

Ohio University. History of Ohio University. Retrieved May 7, 2010http://www.youtube.com/watch?v=CKaUklUloSI

Ohio University. Lindley Hall. Retrieved April 30, 2010, from http://www.ohio.edu/athens/bldgs/lindley.html

Ohio University. Putnam Hall. Retrieved April 30, 2010, from http://www.ohio.edu/athens/bldgs/putnam.html

Ohio University. Tupper Hall. Retrieved April 30, 2010, from http://www.ohio.edu/athens/bldgs/tupper.html

Smith, J. C. (1997) "Paramuthia Two Centuries of Freemasonry in Athens, Ohio". Athens, Ohio: Union Printing Company

Wikipedia. Benjamin Tupper. Retrieved April 30, 2010, from http://en.wikipedia.org/wiki/Benjamin_Tupper

Wikipedia. Ohio Company of Associates. Retrieved May 7, 2010, from http://en.wikipedia.org/wiki/Ohio_Company_of_Associates

Wikipedia. Rufus Putnam. Retrieved May 5, 2010, from http://en.wikipedia.org/wiki/Rufus_Putnam

12

Garments of the High Priest

JEFFREY M. WILLIAMSON

{Presented at the Joint Meeting of the Thomas Smith Webb Chapter of Research No. 1798, Ohio Chapter of Research, and Western New York Lodge of Research, on October 13, 2023, at the Temple in Lackawanna, New York. Exemplar of costume was RE Keith Poppendeck.}

Companions,

The presentation this evening concerns the vestments (or garments) of the High Priest of the Tabernacle as commanded by the Great I Am and communicated by Moses to the Peoples of the Jewish Nation.

Aaron, was the older brother of Moses, and he was appointed by God to be the first High Priest of the nation of Israel. Three chapters in the Torah (the first five books of the Bible) are devoted to describing his clothing, the elaborate regalia that he wore on all official occasions.

- In Exodus 28, describes the priestly garments.
- In Exodus 39, describes the priestly garments.
- In Leviticus 8, describes how the priestly garments are fitted and worn.

There are five different garments that make up the High Priest's garments. The first is the ephod. "Ephod" isn't a word or a garment that we are very familiar with, but it was quite important in the Old Testament, where it is mentioned many times.

It was the outermost garment, and it resembled an elaborate apron. It came to represent the priesthood itself. Its materials were composed of white linen interwoven with threads of solid gold. Its colors – blue, represented our Lord's heavenly origin; purple, represented his royalty; and scarlet, represented his shed blood.

It had onyx stones, which held the garment together at the shoulders. Not to be confused with the breastplate. On these stones were inscribed the names of the twelve tribes of Israel, reminding us of how our **Lord bears us on His shoulders day and night.**

Underneath this ephod was a blue robe, which is described in this reading of Exodus 28:31-35:

> Make the robe of the ephod entirely of blue cloth, with an opening for the head in its center. There shall be a woven edge like a collar around this opening, so that it will not tear.
> Make pomegranates of blue, purple, and scarlet yarn around the hem of the robe, with gold bells between them. The gold bells and the pomegranates are to alternate around the hem of the robe. Aaron

> must wear it when he ministers. The sound of the bells will be heard when he enters the Holy Place before the LORD and when he comes out, so that he will not die.

Thus endeth the reading.

As mentioned previously, the color blue represents our Lord's heavenly origin. But the most intriguing aspect of this blue robe is that along the hem at the bottom were attached little ornaments:

Pomegranates made out of blue, purple, and scarlet thread, and little bells made out of gold. These bells represent the fact that even when the people could not see him, they could hear him. Even when he was in the Holy of Holies on the Yom Kippur (the Day of Atonement) and out of their vision, they could still hear the High Priest and be reassured. (HP goes to B&J)

What do the pomegranates represent? Pomegranates in the Bible are often a symbol of fruitfulness. As taught in the Fellowcraft's degree, the pomegranate is full of seeds. It has a rough, leathery shell on the outside, and when you split it, you find inside a mass of hundreds of edible seeds.

When the twelve spies ventured into the Promised Land, they returned with armfuls of pomegranates to show how fertile and fruitful the land was.

It was described as a land of fig trees and pomegranates. When King Solomon built the Temple in Jerusalem, he had pomegranates carved into the tops or the capitals of the massive columns. This indicated the fruitfulness of the ministry of the High Priest. (pause HP returns to east)

Beneath the blue robe was a white tunic. It was a spotless white robe of woven fabric, made of the finest quality.

The breastplate (pause) worn by the High Priest in the Holy

Temple of Jerusalem is described in Exodus 28:15-30 let us take heed in this reading of the Book of the Law:

> And thou shalt make a breastplate of judgment, the work of the skillful workman; like the work of the ephod thou shalt make it: of gold, of blue, and purple, and scarlet, and fine twined linen, shalt thou make it.
> Four-square it shall be and double: a span shall be the length thereof, and a span the breadth thereof. And thou shalt set in it, settings of stones, four rows of stones: a row of carnelian, topaz, and smaragd shall be the first row.
> And the second row a carbuncle, a sapphire, and an emerald.
> And the third row a jacinth, an agate, and an amethyst.
> And the fourth row a beryl, and an onyx, and a jasper; they shall be enclosed in gold in their settings.

Thus endeth the reading…

The breastplate was nine inches square and folded double with four rows of three precious stones. Each of the twelve precious stones represented one of the tribes of Israel; thus, every time the High Priest entered the Holy of Holies, he would have the children of Israel on his heart.

What does this speak of but the love that the High Priest and, by extension, God himself, has for His children? Think of what a poignant and perfect picture this is. We are His jewels, and He has us on His heart. A representation of the breastplate is the central element of the jewel of a past high priest!

One of the great mysteries of the Bible is that we do not know for certain how the ancient High Priests used the stones called *Urim* (representing light and excellence) and the *Thummim* (representing perfection and completion). When not in use, the Urim and Thummim were kept in a pocket behind the breastplate.

Some scholars think that the two stones were alike and bore words or symbols for "yes" and "no". When a decision had to be made on a binary question such as "Shall we wage war against the Philistines?" the High Priest would pray and then draw one of the stones from the breastplate's pouch, and it would indicate the answer from God. {HP demonstrates}

God could communicate to the High Priest by causing air currents to flicker the light from the High Priest's candle onto the two sacred jewel stones, and thence reflected upon the breastplate, where they would cause flashes upon the breastplate stones. A flash from each of the two sacred jewel stones onto each of the breastplate stones indicated the particular Hebrew letter engraved upon that respective stone, thereby spelling out words and instructions.

While the Urim and Thummim are very mysterious to us, their meaning is clear: God wants to guide His people. He wants to lead and guide you through this time in your life.

The last item of a High Priest's vestments is his head dress call the mitre

The High Priest's mitre is described in Exodus 28:36-39: A reading from the Book of the Law:

> And thou shalt make a plate of pure gold, and engrave upon it, like the engravings of a signet: Holy to the Lord.
> And thou shalt put it on a thread of blue, and it shall be upon the mitre; upon the forefront of the mitre it shall be.
> And it shall be upon Aaron's forehead, and Aaron shall bear the iniquity committed in the holy things, which the children of Israel shall hallow, even in all their holy gifts; and it shall be always upon his forehead, that they may be accepted before the Lord.
> And thou shalt weave the tunic in chequer work of fine linen, and thou shalt make a mitre of fine linen, and thou shalt make a girdle, the work of the weaver in colors.

The words, "**Holiness to the Lord**", mean that the High Priest was devoted and dedicated exclusively to God.

Duties of the High Priest

The duties of the High Priest of the Temple include attending to the lampstand to ensure that the sanctuary's interior is illuminated all night long and offering incense to provide a fragrant aroma – and his weekly presentation and removal of the twelve loaves from the table of shewbread.

All of these rituals are predicated on the sanctuary being God's dwelling place and are precisely delineated in the Bible and are extravagantly outfitted, worthy of God's earthly manifestation. In so doing, the High Priest was directing God's attention to His people's needs and evoking His acceptance of their tribute – all the while taking care to respect His splendid isolation, **never intruding unannounced.**

The High Priest's role in the daily worship of God, as outlined in the Bible, consists of the royal treatment of, and appeal to, the divine King in His earthly palace. The High Priest is the palace servant, and the garments that he wears are intended not merely to clothe him in "dignity and adornment" but to accomplish one of the essential aims of worship: to call the King's attention to His subjects and their needs.

13

Be Cautious Over Your Words...

MICHAEL D. WEISBERG

{Presented 21 March 2024 at Grand Convocation in Binghamton, NY}

As EA, we are admonished to be "cautious over our words and actions, especially on the subject of Freemasonry," but do we even know what words we are to be cautious over? As part of his program, Past Grand Master Thomas encouraged a very old idea; the Hebrew concept of Tikkun Olam, the healing of the world. In doing this, he recommended a path of civility. His program had as one of its main points "Be Inclusive. Civility knows no ethnicity, no level of leadership, no forum, no religion, no generation, and no bounds. Being inclusive includes everyone. It is about leading and serving for the betterment of mankind."

The language of Freemasonry can sound old-fashioned, complicated, and (in many cases) confusing. To add to this, we have words and phrases that are "secret," but we have already promised not to reveal those.

And then there are the myths and legends. Do we even know enough about those to be cautious? Let's prod in a few places and see what we find:

The English Emulation ritual tells us that a Mason is "Brother to a Prince and fellow to a beggar, if he be found worthy." We must remember that the English class system was, and still can be, very rigid, so this by itself is a VERY bold statement. This is clearly exemplified in our ritual, where our mode of dress upon initiation reflects the removal of external class in exchange for the contemplative symbolism of equality. How many times have we told candidates waiting for their degrees, "Don't worry, we've all been through this."

Our ritual takes us one step further, when in the "Lecture of Reasons", known as the "Whys and Wherefores," that we are told that "Masonry regards no man on account of his worldly wealth or honors." In the words of Dr. Martin Luther King, Jr, "I have a dream that my four little children will one day live in a nation where they will not be judged by the color of their skin, but by the content of their character." In this, Dr. King was speaking to a Masonic ideal. Although never a Freemason in life, Dr. King was made a Mason on sight posthumously by the Prince Hall Grand Master of Georgia as he "lived and espoused the Masonic ideal of meeting on the level."

In the Second Degree we once again encounter this theme, although the words are now addressed to the brother in terms of how Masonry views life in terms of attained wealth. Once again, the lesson of equality speaks in a clear voice. "For here on the broad platform of brotherly love, the high, the low, the rich and the poor may meet with one common purpose: the perpetuation of each other's friendship, and each other's love." As FC, we can now afford some of life's superfluities, but even then, "Although it may be given for some to possess more of the world's goods than others, a man who has his health, strength, and ambition has indeed his plenty." Again, these words are a clear rejection of the differentiation of class within the bounds of Freemasonry.

In the Second Degree charge, we are told once again, as we were in the charge, that there is no higher rank or honor than that of being called "Brother!" It is the rank from which we all derive, and the rank that we return to, even when we lay down our working tools. That name also speaks to our responsibility to one another. We must never forget that when the Holy One, Blessed Be He, asked Cain, "Where is your brother Abel?" and he responded, "Am I my brother's keeper?" that the correct answer to the second question was, and still remains, "Yes!" It is this principle that we are reminded of when we are introduced to by the demand on the first degree, and we are obligated to in the third to "see to the relief of distressed masons, their widows and orphans."

When we reach the Third Degree, there are things even more hidden, yet more wonderful, in that it reflects masonry's utter rejection of class within its membership. It is here that we see how death, the leveler of all, does not distinguish position, class, or title. It is here that we are introduced to the Great-Great Grandson of Cain, the great artificer in metal. <Say the name> His name means Leader in Hebrew. In a way, he demonstrates how one can rise from the depths of a cursed past, no matter how cursed, and climb to be a leader amongst his people. It is an interesting coincidence that his half-brother, Jubal, son of Lamech, was said to be the father of all musicians. This theme can be found in the masonic play "In Defense of the Ruffians", where the brothers are (amongst other things) musicians pressed into the service of the Temple.

But there is a still deeper message hidden in the third degree, and as with all good secrets, it is hidden in plain sight. In a way, it reflects the greatest rejection of social distinction of all, that of parentage.

In the ancient world, much of your life, your social status, and even your name, were tied up in your parentage. For example, my Hebrew name is Michael ben Svi. That is Michael, the son of Harold. King Solomon was Zalman ben Dovid, and Hiram, King of Tyre, was Hiram ben Abibaal. Therein is contained a name, parentage, and some social status. One's parentage was of great importance! In fact, there was no social class lower than the Mumzar, the bastard, where the father was not known. While tribal and religious ancestry was determined by one's mother; all inheritance and social standing were transmitted via the father. In our portrayal of the legend of the third degree, we encounter three main characters: Solomon, the son of David, King of Israel; Hiram, the son of Abibaal, King of Tyre; and Hiram Abif. The appellation "Abif" is Hebrew for "(of) His Father." This is another way of saying that Hiram's paternal ancestry was unknown. Further, he is referred to as "The Widow's Son." This again is an indication that his father was not the husband of his mother, but was unknown. In other words, a bastard child. In Freemasonry, we elevate this lowest of social stations to stand in honor in the presence of kings. In this sense, the raising is the fulfilment of the demand of the first degree. It is to remind us that no matter how lowly our position, we truly are the "brother of a prince and fellow to a beggar if... found worthy."

This should be a lesson to all of us as Freemasons, that no distinction of class, prejudice on the basis of any physical characteristic, or any division within our ranks should ever be permitted. This brings us back to the message of the Trowel. Where, in a united mass, no contention should exist, except that noble contention, or rather emulation of who can best work, and best agree!

14

Ancient Mystery Schools

VICTOR ESCORBORES

{Presented 21 June 2024 in Utica Masonic Temple during St. John's Day weekend}

This is a brief paper on the initiatory process of ancient Kemet and the striking similarities found within our Masonic rituals (I shall use Kemet and Egypt interchangeably as this is the true name of Egypt).

Ritual defines man. For we all have rituals in our daily lives and these ultimately create who we are as Men in this world. These patterns of activity, such as the proverbial defecation, showering and shaving routine, or that of awakening, praying, exercising, and working, eating, then watching television and sleeping routine, are rituals we are all too familiar with. These routine rituals correspond to the profane world. Ritual/routine not only defines the profane it too defines a Free and Accepted Mason and all brethren of the Noble Craft.

The most meaningful and important aspect of our Fraternal brotherhood are the Rites and the order in which they are performed, thus defining our Masonic ritual. The ritual is indeed that which binds us into the Mystic Tie. As is stated in the Degree work of the Symbolic Lodge, we do that "which all brethren have done who have gone this way before me." The initiatory process and the corresponding rites are indeed what make a Mason, a Mason as such. We as Brothers have all undertaken in some form or fashion, being entered on the rolls as Apprentices, thus becoming Neophytes on a new journey of self-discovery. We all have, in some form, been passed to a Fellow of the Craft, a novice who knows yet is still grasping to fully understand.

We have all been Raised to the Sublime Degree of Master Mason, becoming an Adept who knows that he knows and truly understands that he indeed knows not.

As is often quoted of Plato, as said by Scocrates "scio me nihil scire", as found in Apologia, (trans. 1961/ca. 399 BCE, 21d) "I do not think that I know what I do not know (I know, I know nothing)". Such is the mind of a true Master Mason.

The constant practice of a thing forms a habit. I would safely surmise that it is our habits which form us and create our personalities and beings. Whether these be habits of action and behavior and thought, they define a man and Mason. We as Masons are in the habit of continually attempting to perfect ourselves, ever attempting to become the "Human image of a Masons God" (Standard Work and Lectures 2019 pg. 309).

These lofty goals and principles of self-elevation and perfection via rituals of initiation are found throughout the Ancient world.

As man, in his attempt to understand his place in the cosmos and, ergo, his relationship to the Great Cause, he has undergone Initiation, Passing, and Raising of some variable form since time immemorial and truly forever.

I will focus on Kemet, which translates as the land of the Black soil and Black peoples. This is due to the inundation of the Nile, which produced nutrient-rich black soil, as well as to the highly melanated peoples who were natives of the great empire. There are some interesting parallels found within the forms, rites, and ceremonies of the ancient priesthoods of Kemet, and our own three Degrees of the Freemasonry within the Grand Lodge of New York.

Masons have always looked to Kemet as the greatest builders and Architects of our time. This is of course forever memorialized by the Great Pyramids which have withstood the test of time. Kemet/ Egypt has always been considered the birthplace of the Mysteries (Albert Mackey Encyclopedia of Freemasonry 2nd edition pg 232). We find there the first initiation ceremonies of the ancient world. Masons take their main symbolism from the building of the Temple of God by Solomon. From Egypt comes this wisdom for "Moses was learned in all the Wisdom of Egypt " and Moses is the progenitor of the tabernacle and that divine Law which gave way to the building of the Temple of Solomon, which is said to have been a representation of said tabernacle. I shall digress momentarily to elaborate on the significance and probable origins of the formation of our Symbolic temple, we shall then again come to Egypt.

Let us begin with a brief overview of what our ritual is and what the Great Light says regarding the Temple. What is a Lodge? We learn from our First Degree Historic Lecture that a Lodge may be defined as a certain number of Freemasons duly assembled. Where did our ancient brethren hold their lodges? They were held in high hills or low valleys, this intimates that our brethren held gatherings outside in nature. What is the Form of a Lodge? The form of a Lodge is oblong, in length from east to west, in breadth between North and South, as high as heaven, and as deep as from the surface to the center. Here we are acquainted with the idea that a Lodge has the form of being oblong but is not restricted to a material edifice. The covering of a Lodge is said to be the Starry Decked heaven, which intimates that in reality there is no cover. The Lodge is indeed as expansive as the heavens themselves, where, of course, all good Masons hope to arrive. We further gather from the ritual of the First Degree that the Lodge is situated due East and West because King Solomon's Temple was so situated.

With the aid of the Great Light we can read in Kings and Chronicles the description of Solomon's

Temple, and I highly suggest that in your leisure hours please do read the Great Light on this subject so as to get a better understanding of its extraordinary beauty. It is most important to note that Solomon's Temple had a holy place and a Holy of Holies. Moses erected the Tabernacle in the wilderness and Solomon erected the permanent Temple. Our ritual explains that King Solomon's Temple is said to have been a representative of that Tabernacle.

According to Brother Albert Mackey, the Hebrews called a temple Beth, which literally signifies a house or dwelling. This is an actual material structure, as well as Hecal, which means a palace. These two methods of identifying the place of the manifestation of the Most Holy recall that the Lodge/Temple is both a physical and non-physical thing. Hecal-Yehova was the structure of the edifice. The room- Beth. Yehovah is the spiritual emanation of the divine. Mackey further states, " that they seem to have had two ideas in reference to a temple. When they called it Beth Jehovah, or the house of Jehovah; they referred to the continued presence of God in it; and when they called it Hecal-jehovah, or the palace of Jehovah; they referred to the splendor of the edifice which was selected as his residence (Albert Mackey Encyclopedia of Freemasonry 2nd edition pgs 766-767).

Moses was learned in the wisdom of Kemet. "And Moses was learned in all the wisdom of the Egyptians, and was mighty in words and deeds" (Acts 7:22, King James Bible). It naturally follows that in his construction of the tabernacle, he implemented what he had gleaned from the priest of Kemit. One can then conclude that since Solomon's temple was a representative of Mose's tabernacle, then it too must have had the elements which can be traced to Kemet.

The Egyptian Temple was the real archetype of the Mosaic tabernacle, as it was also the archetype of the temple of Jerusalem. The direction of an Egyptian temple was usually from east to west, the entrance being at the east. It was a quadrangular building, much longer than its width, and was situated in the western part of a sacred enclosure. The approach through this enclosure to the temple proper was frequently by a double row of 796 temple sphinxes. In front of the entrance were a pair of tall obelisks, which were reminiscent of the two pillars at the porch of Solomon's Temple. The temple was divided into a spacious hall, the sanctuary, where the great body of the worshippers assembled, and beyond it, in the western extremity, was the cell or sekos, equivalent to the Jewish Holy of Holies, into which the priests only entered; and in the remotest part, behind a curtain, appeared the image of the God seated on his shrine, or the sacred animal which represented him.

Grecian Temples, like the Egyptian and the Hebrew, were placed within an enclosure, which was separated from the profane land around it, in early times, by ropes, but afterwards by a wall. The temple was usually quadrangular, although some were circular in form. It was divided into two parts — the pronaos, porch or vestibule, and the naos, or cell. In this latter part, the statue of the god was placed, surrounded by a balustrade.

In temples connected with the Mysteries, the cell was called the adytum, and to it only the priests and the initiates had access; and we learn from Pausanias that various stories were related of calamities that had befallen persons who had unlawfully ventured to cross the threshold. Vitruvius says that the entrance of Greek temples was always towards the west ; but this statement is contradicted by the appearance of the temples still partly existing in Attica, Ionia, and Sicily. Roman Temples, after they emerged from their primitive simplicity, were constructed much upon the model of the Grecian. There were the same vestibule and cells, or adytum, borrowed, as with the Greeks, from the holy and the most holy place of the Egyptians. Vitruvius (trans. 1914/ca. 15 BCE) further states in Book IV, that the entrance of a Roman temple was, if possible, to the west, so that the worshippers, when they offered prayers or sacrifices, might look towards the east; but this rule was not always observed.

It thus appears, notwithstanding what Montfaucon says to the contrary (Montfaucon, 1719/1721, Vol. 2, Book 2, Chap. 2), that the Egyptian form of a temple was the type from which all other nations borrowed their idea. This Egyptian form of a temple was borrowed by the Jews/Hebrews, and with modifications also adopted by the Greeks and Romans, whence it passed over into modern Europe. This idea of a separation into a Holy and a Most Holy of Holies-place has been preserved everywhere.

The same idea is maintained in the construction of Masonic Lodges, which are but imitations, in spirit, of the ancient temples. There has however, been a transposition of parts, the Most Holy place, which with the Egyptians and the Jews was in the west, being placed in Lodges in the east. The Hebrew idea was undoubtedly borrowed from the Egyptian.

Now that the lineage of even our symbolic temple formation is established to be from Kemet. Let us continue with the initiatory process. In Kemit, the initiatory process was such that the initiate had to prove his loyalty and ability to maintain secrecy. He was required to undergo a period of purification and to undergo a strict vegetarian diet. We find a similarity in that our candidate must be of the tongue of good report.

The Mystery schools consisted of two types: the outer or Lesser Mysteries, which consisted of the Mysteries of Isis; and the inner or Greater Mysteries, which consisted of the Mysteries of Serapis and Osiris. (Albert Mackey Encyclopedia of Freemasonry 2nd edition pg 232).

The conductor of the Candidate who spoke for him was Anubis. Apuleius wrote, “a god serves as a messenger between the world above and the infernal world” (Max Guilmont, “The Initiatory Process in Ancient Egypt”, pg 15). This can be parallel to the conductor speaking for the validity of the initiate and candidate at every instance of his degree work. We find that all initiates had to go about a long crossing or journey under the guidance of the conductor-Anubis and then entrance into the sanctuary (Max Guilmont, "The Initiatory Process in Ancient Egypt", pg 17).

The Kematian first degree was that of Isis Mysteries. She represented Nature. Apuleus having been initiated into the lesser first degree says " the priest .. took my hand, brought me into the inner recesses of the sanctuary, clothed in a new linen garment". Here we find the initiatory candidate clothed in white as we find in our own degree work. White or linen has always been a representation of purity of purpose in mind, body, and intent. Our masonic Apron is also handed down to us from Kemet and the ancient builders of the Pyramids. The ancient ceremonial cloaks consisted of the sacred triangle of Egypt, which was the Symbol of the all-seeing eye of Horus, known as the Eye of Heaven, interpreted as the Sun God. (Rodgers, 2010).

The second degree or that of the Mysteries of Serapis are said to have been preparatory for the last degree — that of Osiris. The formal training of the Neophyte consisted of what is popularly known as the Trivium and Quadrivium. The Neophyte was educated in Grammar. Arithmetic, Rhetoric, Dialectic, Geometry , Astronomy and Music. To be allowed into the higher degree the initiate had to become acquainted with the 42 books of Hermes (James, 1954, pg. 135)

In the third degree of the Osiris Mysteries, the lessons of death and resurrection were taught symbolically. The lessons of the mysteries of Osiris are strikingly similar to those of the Hiramic legend. The Osirian legend goes as follows: Osiris the wise King of Kemit left his Kingdom in the charge of his wife Isis, for he was to travel three years to give the knowledge of Kemet to other civilizations. We find a traveler, Osiris, going from East to West to spread and receive the light of knowledge. This is highly reminiscent of the very nature of our ritual.

Typhon, his brother, formed a conspiracy to overtake the throne upon his arrival. Typhon created a casket of gold and proclaimed any who would fit in it would be given it. Osiris, wanting to appease his brother, laid in it. Thus, the coffin was shut and he was thrown into the river, where he was left to die. There are other variations of this legendary tale in which Typhon, identified as Set, cut his brother up into 12 pieces plus his member, scattering his remains in the Nile. In either tale, Isis the wife goes in search of the remains on a westerly course, she represents nature, ultimately finds the body in the coffin (or the various body parts scattered throughout the lands) and regenerates and brings to life a new Osiris. The death search for and ultimate discovery of the body of Osiris and the sufferings and death and ultimate resurrection of Osiris were the great Mystery of the Egyptian initiatory rite. The similarities and parallels are quite evident even to the newly Raised Mason.

The initiate is raised to his new life by the lion's paw in the mysteries of Kemet as well.

We further find In some of the sculptures left by the Egyptians to illustrate the rites of the Egyptian Mysteries, the candidate is shown lying on a couch shaped like a lion from which he is being raised from the dead level to a living perpendicular. The bas-reliefs at Denderah make this very plain, though they represent the god Osiris being raised. The candidate is raised with and by the Ankh, known as the Crux Ansata. The Ankh is a symbol of life-giving power. Many a masonic writer, Albert Pike included, has found that the Crux Ansata was the first form of that Lion's Paw. The Lion's paw may therefore be interpreted as a symbol of life-giving power. (https://www.sacred-texts.com/mas/syma/syma53.htm Symbolical Masonry, by H.L. Haywood, [1923] Chapter 49 pages 279-280)

In Spell 175 of the Book of the Dead (Faulkner, trans. 1972/ ca. 1550 BCE), or the Book of Coming to Day from Night, as it is more accurately titled, an excerpt detailing the entrance of the candidates into the mystery school. Here, the candidate converses with the GAOTU Atum.

> Man: O Atum,
> Why have I traveled the desert? the fact is that there is no water, No breeze.
> (this land) is deep, deep
> Dark , Dark,
> without limits or frontiers!
> Atum: There though shall live with thou heart in peace
> Man: But one over there can not satisfy love!
> God: it is there I have placed the powers of Mind
> instead of love,
> and peace of mind instead of bread and bear..
> Man: and what will be my lifespan
> Atum: Thou shall live for millions and millions of years. (Thy life) shall last for millions and millions of years)!

Finally Here we find the initiate being told of the need for death as one of the inescapable processes of life and becoming aware of the immortality of the soul.

To my Brethren, I turn to you, the skilled craftsman, to decipher if these similarities are but mere coincidence. Although I may be somewhat proficient in our lectures of the degree work, I claim no perfect understanding of other subjects to which I am but a novice seeking blindly. I am grateful to be able to share my thoughts via this brief discourse on the Ancient Mystery schools of

Kemet and their probable relation to our work. I look forward to the wisdom of future generations to find ever more light on this topic.

Yours in service with Light and Love;

Brother Victor Escorbores

BIBLIOGRAPHY

Faulkner, R. O. (Trans.). (1972). "The ancient Egyptian book of the dead". British Museum Publications. (Original work published ca. 1550 BCE).

Grand Lodge of Free and Accepted Masons of the State of New York. (2019). "Standard work and lectures."

Haywood, H. L. (n.d.). "Symbolical masonry. Internet Sacred Text Archive". www.sacred-texts.com (Original work published 1923).

"The Holy Bible, King James version". (2017). King James Bible Online. https://www.kingjamesbibleonline.org (Original work published 1611).

James, G. G. M. (1954). "Stolen legacy: Greek philosophy is stolen Egyptian philosophy". Philosophical Library.

Montfaucon, B. (1721–1725). "Antiquity explained, and represented in sculptures" (D. Humphreys, Trans.; Vol. 2). Printed by J. Tonson and J. Watts. (Original work published 1719).

Plato. (1961). "The collected dialogues of Plato, including the letters" (E. Hamilton & H. Cairns, Eds.; L. Cooper et al., Trans.). Princeton University Press. (Original works published ca. 399–347 BCE).

Rodgers, J. M. (2010, August 1). "Badge of a Mason". California Lodge of Research Short Talk Bulletin, 1. California Lodge of Research.

Vitruvius Pollio. (1914). "Vitruvius: The ten books on architecture" (M. H. Morgan, Trans.). Harvard University Press. (Original work published ca. 15 BCE).

15

Masonic Wages

GREGORY D. MACLEOD

{Presented 21 June 2024 in Utica Masonic Temple during St. John's Day weekend. Companion MscCleod is a member of Highland Chapter No.52.}

The concept of wages comes up throughout our several Masonic degrees. It is first presented explicitly at the conclusion of the Middle Chamber Lecture of the Fellow craft degree. It comes up again, albeit briefly, at the opening and closing of a Master Mason Lodge, as paying the craft their wages is one of the duties which is delegated to the Senior Warden's station. Tangentially, in the Entered Apprentice Degree, there is a brief reference to a penny. Despite these various references to items of monetary value within the first three degrees, the concept of wages is explored, perhaps at its greatest depth, in the Mark Master Degree of the

Royal Arch, where one actually learns the proper way to receive said wages, should any be due to him, as well as what the proper wage for a craftsman should be.

The astute observer will notice there is a subtle difference in the wages paid. In the Fellowcraft degree, one receives physical items, and are told what they represent, whereas in the Mark Master, the coin of the realm is used as a means of exchange. Are there perhaps reasons for such an apparent discrepancy between these two degrees? What was used as a medium of exchange in ancient times? And most importantly, how does that relate to our modern-day notions of money, credit, and value?

The first known coins, that is to say pieces of metal of a known weight and compositions, embossed with a seal or other distinguishing feature, "only" date back to around 630 BC[i]. Prior to that, gold, silver, or other precious metal was simply weighed out with a scale. Thus, a Jewish Shekel, as referred to over fifty times throughout the Torah (Gn 20:16, Ex 30:13, etc.) was a unit of measure[ii], and not a coin per se.

Going back even further, physical goods would have been bartered for others, as was customary in Ancient Egypt.[iii] For much of their early history, the Jewish people were nomads. From the time of Abraham through to Jacob, later known as Israel (Gn 32:28), were for the majority of that time without the permanent homeland promised to them by God, and traveled back and forth between Palestine and Mesopotamia several times over before finally arriving in Egypt to escape famine. It was a barter economy with sheep, oxen, grain, wine, oil, and even salt used as mediums of exchange.

When they were finally liberated by Moses, the Hebrews once again found themselves as nomads, wandering through the desert.

They would have traveled with their livestock and carried their possessions on their person. They even had precious metals, "given" to them by the Egyptians, prior to their departure (Ex 12:35).

Thus, they were able to form the Ark of the Covenant per the Lord's instructions, including overlaying it with pure Gold (Ex 37:2). They also had access to Bronze (a mixture of Copper and Tin), Brass (a mixture of Copper and Zinc), Silver and Lead, for they used these metals to fabricate many of the vessels and other accouterments that would travel with Mose's tabernacle, and ultimately be placed withing the first Temple of Solomon many centuries later.

Scripture informs us that the concept of a "Temple Tax" was first prescribed by Moses (Ex 30:11-16) where every male over twenty years old was to donate a half shekel as an *offering to the LORD.* The obligation of the Mark Master refers to the Jewish Half Shekel as being equal to a quarter of a dollar. It further states that the wages of a Fellowcraft are "one penny a day", thus 25 days, or approximately one month's worth of work, goes to the Lord. Recall the Jews of the time followed a lunisolar calendar consisting of 12 months of between 29 and 30 days each.[iv] Subtracting out the sabbath, one arrives at 25 to 26 days of work done in a given month.

Even today, tithing is typically set at 10% of one's income, which hearkens back to the original promise of Jacob to the Lord at Beth-El, after his vision of that ladder extending from Earth to Heaven. (Gn 28:22) where he promised to return "*a tenth part to you [The Lord] without fail."* It is further reinforced in Dt 14:22-29, which specifically mentions that measures of corn, wine, and oil, as well as the firstborn of the flock, as items appropriate to offer for yearly tithing. These tithes were to be stored for use by the Levites (who were without inheritance or property due to their priestly function within the community), the stranger, the fatherless, and the widow.

By all accounts, through the rule of Solomon, the people of the time used talents of metal, be it gold or silver, as their medium of exchange, and coins as we know them in the modern sense had not yet been developed or widely promulgated. By the time of the exile, 538 BC, coins were just coming into fashion, being first used in ancient Lydia, in current-day Turkey.[v] Certainly by the end of the exile period, 333 BC when they returned to their homeland, the Persian empire would have been circulating coins as an exchange of value.[vi]

Thus, the penny a day received by the craftsman in the Mark Master degree may well be symbolic of the second temple, rather than the first. Erection of the first temple commenced in 950 BC[vii], before the usage of coins as we know them today. Although most of the workmen were conscripted from the neighboring tribes whom David had conquered, according to 2 Chronicles 2:9, Solomon offered to pay the woodcutters supplied by Hiram, King of Tyre, in equal measures of wheat and barley plus wine and oil. Thus, during the first temple period, the concepts of coinage had not yet caught on!

The Mark Master being a bit of an amalgamation between the Fellowcarft and Master Masons Degrees, it makes some sense that the time frame would shift. In the first section of the Degree, one is clearly operating as a Fellowcraft in the quarries for the purpose of constructing the first temple. This is evident by the nature of the unfinished piece that was discovered, and the individual who wrought it. But towards the end of the degree, when clothed as a

Master Mason, you find yourself for want of a token, and are further informed the wages of a Fellowcraft are "a penny a day" to enable one to "procure the necessities of life" this is clearly coin of the realm, which puts us historically at the building of the second temple.

So what can this teach us? First, the wages of a Mason are many and varied. We must provide for each other's needs either directly (physical goods) or indirectly (money or other forms of exchange). Given the importance Masonry puts on Charity, it makes sense that the importance of giving what we have to those in need is expounded time and time again throughout the Masonic degrees, particularly in both the Entered Apprentice Degree and again in the Mark Master Degree. Although Masons are under no direct obligation to Tithe, it's alluded to in the Mark Master obligation, for the price of one's Mark is equivalent to the Temple Tax superscribed in Mosaic Law as noted earlier.

Note the progression here. In the Entered Apprentice degree, we are admonished in order to teach us to be charitable. In the Fellowcraft Degree, we receive wages to provide for not only our basic needs, but also our material comforts. In the Mark Master degree, we are encouraged to materially support any brother who offers his mark as a pledge.

But weather goods, currency or even bitcoin, value is a relative proposition. In today's society, currency is fiat, backed by nothing except one's faith in the system as a whole. Each country's government (or a block of countries, as is the case in the European Union) has a central bank that issues currency. Those bills and coins are backed by nothing more than the credit of the nation(s) themselves. No physical gold or silver or other precious metal backs the modern money supply. Thus, money is based on trust.

We have faith that our money has value since society has deemed it so, and hope that it will retain a portion of that value in the future, inflation notwithstanding. Perhaps this explains the rise of cryptocurrency such as Bitcoin. Value is what you make of it, be it seashells, embossed pieces of metal, printed pieces of paper, or even bytes and bits stored in an electronic ledger on computers spread far and wide. Faith in our fellow man to provide for us fairly based on our labors, and hope that others will see value in whatever medium of exchange we utilize, are central to any monetary system functioning successfully.

The good book has many lessons about wealth. St. Paul tells us that "the *love* of money is the root of all kinds of evil" (1 Tm 6:10) and reminds us of the importance of Charity. Jesus himself states that Mathew XX is the parable of the vineyard workers and teaches us that we should not be jealous of how others earn their keep, but be satisfied with our own endeavors.

Probably the biggest "Value" of being a Master Mason, or a Royal Arch Mason, is the ability to freely travel. Remember it is the internal, not the external. We are not defined by our worldly wealth or honors. How we live, how we treat others, is the measure by which we are ultimately judged. Living uprightly and charitably is more important than how much "stuff" we have or how many zeros are in our bank accounts.

[i] https://www.worldhistory.org/article/1793/the-invention-of-the-first-coinage-in-ancient-lydi/

[ii] https://www.jewishvirtuallibrary.org/weights-measures-and-coins-of-the-biblical-and-talmudic-periods

[iii] Serge Svizzero, Clement Tisdell. "Barter and the Origin of

Money and Some Insights from the Ancient Palatial Economies of Mesopotamia"

[iv] https://www.britannica.com/topic/Jewish-religious-year

[v] https://www.worldhistory.org/article/1793/the-invention-of-the-first-coinage-in-ancient-lydi/

[vi] https://coinweek.com/ancient-coins-wealth-persian-empire/

[vii] https://www.jewishvirtuallibrary.org/the-first-temple-solomon-s-temple

16

Symbolism of the Altars of the Royal Arch

GREGORY D. MACLEOD

{Presented June 2025 in Utica Masonic Temple during St. John's Day weekend}

Background: While preparing to confer the Holy Royal Arch Degree for the first time as High Priest, I noticed, for the first time, that the Captain of the Host, rather than the High Priest, confers the obligation. I called my District Deputy in a bit of a panic, afraid that a typo had somehow made its way into our Standard Ritual. He assured me that the book was correct... but why would a lower-ranking officer be left with such an important task?

As luck would have it this topic came up again briefly during a subsequent Grand Lecturer Convention in 2025. RE James Gregg was discussing the mechanism by which the furnishings of the Lodge are moved from the triangular altar in the East to the Rectangular or square alter in the West, and the role of the Captain of the Host in the degree conferral came up.

Here is another detail that seems to have alluded me! Two Altars? And why WAS the Captain of the Host left to confer the degree? Perhaps taking a one-day class was ill-advised all those years ago, but I had seen a handful of Royal Arch Degrees conferred since by competent degree teams, including the Grand Line itself, and never recalled TWO altars. Hadn't the High Priest ALWAYS conferred the obligation? Clearly, I was misremembering my own experience. Thus began my research into what became this paper I now present.

The Royal Arch Degree has several unique aspects that warrant special consideration. First, the perambulations, with the exception of the initial circuit, are done AFTER rather than BEFORE the obligation. Second, the Caption of the Host, not the High Priest, confers the obligation. Third, unlike all of the other degrees in Masonry (up to this point at least) there is not one but TWO altars used; the triangular altar in the East and Square or at times Rectangular altar in the West. To traverse between these two altars, one must necessarily pass through the three veils, and at each be duly examined before they can reach the threshold of the Sanctuary. With such rich symbolism that hits on so many levels, let us once again travel from the West to the East, and unpack the deeper meaning of the altars used in this profound degree.

First, before we even get to the altar the candidates always three, no more, no less, who, guided by the Principal Sojourner, enter the lodge "under the living arch", where each is made to stoop low. The Biblical passage "*He who humbles himself will be exulted*"[i] is simultaneously recited. Although this unique entrance is not referred to anywhere else in the ceremony, we will tie it in by the end of this presentation, along with the two altars and the candidate's journey, in order to unlock what is in my opinion one of the principal secrets of this degree.

The principal sojourner then guides the candidates through the first perambulation. As with much of our ritual, this passage is derived from Biblical sources. Specifically from the Prophet Isiah[ii] who was foreshadowing that Great Patron Saint of Masonry, John the Baptist, who cited Isiah's prophecy in reference to his ministry[iii]. This is a fundamental point. The principal sojourner, representative of John the Baptist, is guiding the three candidates to a yet unknown destination with the promise of being Exalted to the most sublime Degree of the Royal Arch. Let us continue our journey and discover where we are heading.

After this unique entrance, we make, as in the preceding degrees, a certain number of perambulations. Although this should be familiar, there is a unique difference pertaining to this march around the room. Only the first perambulation is done prior to the obligation, at which point we come to the first altar, placed in the West. This is the traditional four-sided altar we are accustomed to from our craft lodges. Although in many chapters this altar is Rectangular, the ritual of the Grand Chapter of the State of New York calls for it to be a square[iv]. The noted Masonic author Mackey agrees, stating, *"The form of a Masonic altar should be a cube, about three feet high, and of corresponding proportions as to length and width, having, in imitation of the Jewish altar, four horns, one at each corner."*[v]

The book of Exodus describes several altars which were made for the original tabernacle in the desert, which was the precursor to Kings Solomon's Temple on Mount Moriah in Jerusalem.

Among which is a rectangular table, 2 cubits in length by x 1 cubit in breadth, on which the shewbread was placed and was located OUTSIDE the veils and TWO square altars, one five cubits by five cubits square, the other one cubit by one cubit square for the purpose of burning incense, to be located INSIDE the Holy of Holies.[vi] Granted, Masonic Ritual and the Holy Bible don't always need to fully align, but it is curious that scripturally, the rectangular altar is outside the Sanctum Sanctorum, whereas the square altars are inside.

In part, this hearkens back to the concept of the rough vs. perfect ashlar from the lecture of the first degree. The rough ashlar is generally depicted as rectangular stone, whereas the perfect ashlar is, or ought to be, represented by a cube. The rough ashlar is a reminder of our rude, imperfect state. As we chip away our rough edges, we discover the perfected stone within.

Similarly, the floor of a Lodge is twice as long as it is wide. The length being longer than the breadth suggests an imbalance, and alludes to a certain tension, a push and pull which pervades our life experience. The form of a lodge alludes to the original tabernacle built by Moses, which was a rectangular tent, 45 feet long by 15 ft wide. It should be noted that this original tabernacle was further divided into two separate sections, a 30 ft by 15 ft space (The Holy Place) followed by a smaller 15 ft square space (The Most Holy Place).[vii],[viii] This additional chamber was set apart; the inner sanctum where the Holy of Holies resides, which was accessed by the High Priest once a year on the day of Atonement.[ix]

Contrast with the perfect ashlar. A Cube. Smooth. Square. Balanced. Perfection. By using a square altar, we allude to the fact that we are perfected on the earthly plane, but have not yet passed the veils to gain admission to the spiritual plane within the Sanctum Sanctorum. That only comes after journeying across the veils and at each station being duly examined. Such is our time on Earth. Buffeted by trials and tribulations, seeking to moor ourselves in that peaceful harbor, searching for stability. It's a quest for God, the divine, to perfect within ourselves that rough stone and by slowly chipping away, making it more uniform, more square. And although our journey at times is arduous, if we persist, we will be rewarded. Recall that in the Mark Master degree the Whiteness of the Keystone alludes to a certain passage of Scripture, "*To he that overcommeth, I will give to eat of the hidden manna, and I give him a white stone, and in the Stone a new name is written which no man knoweth, save the one receiving it*"[x]

The rectangle and the number four are symbolic of Earth, the terrestrial.[xi] Pythagoras is to have said that it contains all the mysteries of nature.[xii] Four sides, six faces, emblematic of the six days of creation and the four ancient classical elements which appear in the creation narrative in the book of Genesis.[xiii] If we consider the four ancient elements, earth is the FOURTH of the elements to come to be. For it is true that although in the beginning God created the heaven and the Earth, initially the Earth was without form and void. Although the materials of creation existed, the clay had not yet been formed into *terra firma*. The spirit of God (Air) preexisted even creation itself, as did the waters which were ultimately separated by the almighty into the sky above and the seas below. Thus Water and Air precluded Earth. Light was the first creation, analogous to the ancient element fire, which gives forth both light and heat. Then the firmament was then created to keep the waters above (the blue skies of haven) and the waters below apart. It was not until the third day that Earth came to be as the waters of the seas receded. Thus, Earth being the fourth and final element, the number four is an "earthy" sign.

It also symbolizes stability, structure, and balance[xiv]. There are four cardinal directions and four cardinal virtues that guide us. Even in that original tabernacle, the tent erected by Moses, each of the four principal tribes of Israel, Dan, Reuben, Ephraim, and Judah, took positions North, South, West, and East of this tabernacle.[xv] It should be noted that Judah is in the East. This is another clue as to where the journey is leading.

One can take this a step further and relate it to the four fixed signs of the Zodiac[xvi], the Leo in the Northeast, alludes to the ancient element Fire, represented by the Lion, Scorpio in the Northwest is indicative of Water, the Aquarius in the Southwest representing Air, and the Taurus in the Southeast, symbolizing the Earth.[xvii] If we rotate the positions of these fixed signs clockwise by 45 degrees, we end up with Leo the Lion in the East, Scorpio analogous to the Eagle in the North, Aquarius, the Air sign, in the West, indicative of that Miraculous East Wind referenced in the first degree historical lecture, and Taurus in the South.

Finally, if we examine the symbology on the Royal Arch Banner, we find the symbol for each of the four principal tribes represented, The Lion, Man, The Ox, and The Eagle. [xviii] Not only did Ezekiel see these four creatures in his vision[xix], these also allude to the four authors of the Gospels of the Christian New Testament, Mathew, Mark, Luke, and John[xx].

Four is balance. Earthly. For signs of the zodiac. Four cardinal directions. Four ancient elements. Four cardinal virtues (fortitude, prudence, temperance, and justice) It is upon this four-sided altar that the candidate is obligated as a Royal Arch Mason, and forevermore will be known not as a Brother but as a Companion. Let us continue the journey.

Only after the obligation is conferred is are the candidates allowed to continue their perambulations; all occurring in the west around the four-sided altar. It should be noted that, unlike prior Degrees the candidate remains hoodwinked after the obligation and is led by the Principal Sojourner by a way he knows not. The scripture lessons in each perambulation tell the story of the Jewish people, with a special focus on Moses and his encounter with God in the form of a burning bush. This encounter with the divine is so profound that the candidate's hoodwink is not removed until after the second perambulation, so that he may behold the bush and the presence of God within, for himself.

The fourth perambulation concludes the Moses story as he leads his people to the doorstep of the Promised Land, the final three referring to the passage of time between the first and second temples. In summary these perambulations lay bare the struggle of the Jewish people, from Moses leading them through the wilderness to the footsteps of the Promised Land, Joshua leading them across the Jordan and into the land of Canaan, the rise and subsequent fall of the Jewish Empire, which led to the destruction of King Solomon's Temple at the hand of the Babylonians over 400 years after its erection, and its subsequent rebuilding 70 plus years thereafter when the children of Israel, under the auspices of the Persian King Cyrus the great, allowed them to return to their homeland. We, too, as Royal Arch Masons, are making an equally arduous journey from the Terrestrial to the Celestial, from knowledge to understanding, from a Master Mason to a Royal Arch Mason with all of the privileges and responsibility that such a station holds.

The triangular altar in the East and the Square altar in the West are physically separated by the veils. At each station we are tested. The words of each veil are significant. Shem, Ham, and Japtheh, Noah's sons, who helped build the original ark, which carried them safely through the flood waters. Moses, Aholiab and Bezalel, who helped construct the tabernacle which housed the second ark, which stored the tablets of ten commandments and the manna which fed the Israelites, and Zerubabel, Jeshua, and Hagga,i who were instrumental in rebuilding the temple and who, in the context of the degree, rediscovered the true Master's Word.

These veils lead to the Sanctum Sanctorum, the Holy of Holies, where the Ark of the Covenant, in which the Spirit of God himself resides. This explains why the Captain of the Host, and not the High Priest, administers the obligation. The Grand Council is comprised of the three elective officers, the High Priest, the King and the Tribe. They remain in the East and only descend into the Sanctum Sanctorum, to raise and subsequently lower the Royal Arch at the Opening and Closing respectfully. Otherwise they are set apart, on the dais above and watching over the proceedings below. If we view the west as the terrestrial and the east as the spiritual, with the veils being the divide between the two, guarded by three Masters plus the Royal Arch Captain in front of the white sheet that leads to the Sanctum Sanctorum. The Grand Council, representing the spiritual realm, are physical separated from the Terrestrial by the veils. They, although three distinct officers, act in concert as one body. A Trinitarian Christian should recognize the deeper symbolism this alludes to. Three distinct persons (Father, Son and Spirit) yet somehow one.

If this spiritual dimension needs to remain in the East, then those left on the terrestrial plane are left to traverse from west to east to rediscover their spiritual dimension, by passing through the veils, guided by the principal sojourner.

It should be noted that the Captain of the Host, after the opening, takes up his seat in lodge in the West, occupying the Chair of the Senior Warden. And, as we know from our craft lodges, if the Worshipful Master is absent WHO is left to preside? The Senior Warden. THIS is why the Captain of the Host administers the obligation. HE has been left on the terrestrial plane. The Worshipful Master is in the realm of the spiritual. Represented by the priest, scribe and king, alluding to our call to be priest, prophet and kings Now the priest and king are straightforward, but the scribe less so. But who wrote down the words of the prophets? Tradition tells us that the four major prophets wrote down their own books[xxi], thus the Scribe is representative of the Prophet. Scribes were also called on to write, read and at times interpret the law.[xxii]

Deviating from biblical tradition, the altar in the East is a triangle rather than a square. Why? The number three throughout the ages has been a significant number. When I was taking theology in High School, I remember the teacher going off on a tangent about numerology, and to him at least, the number three signified importance.

The ritual tells us that the triangular altar is emblematical of the three essential attributes of deity. Omnipresence, Omniscience, and Omnipotence are all present in one God. The equilateral triangle, being symmetrical on all sides, was adopted by the ancients as a symbol of Deity and the three phases of time; past, present, and future. Our ritual teaches us that for the Hebrews, the first letter of the tetragrammaton, Yod, placed within a triangle, is symbolic of that great and sacred name which was for them, and is now, ineffable.

Three has a deep significance throughout Masonry. Three degrees, three principal officers, three steps, three columns, three ornaments, three greater and three lesser lights, three movable and three immovable jewels, three principal tenants, three rounds of Jacob's ladder alluding to the three spiritual virtues, faith hope and charity. Three working tools of a Fellowcraft, three ancient orders of classical architecture — the Doric, the Ionic, and the Corinthian ; three human senses are a prerequisite to being made a Mason — seeing, hearing, and feeling. Three Grand Masters, three ruffians who accosted GMHA at each of the three gates, and even his body was buried three times between his untimely death and its final interment — once in the rubbish after his murder, then on the brow of a certain hill, and finally a proper interment as close to the Sanctum Sanctorum as Jewish Law would allow.

Throughout our rituals the number THREE comes up time and time again. We necessarily pass through three veils, before entering the Inner Sanctum where the Ark of the Covenant lay, and within the Ark are three precious Items, the Pot of Manna, Arron's Rod and Law; the Stone Tablets which Moses received from the Almighty on Mt. Sinai, written by his own hand, that finger of divinity. Even the True Master's Word, the great and sacred name of God, was split into three syllables, Ja – Ho – Va, such that no one man would pronounce such a sacred name. And of course that which led to the rediscovery of the True Masters Word, the missing vowels that complete the Tetragramatron, Jah – Bel – On, which we recite the opening to commemorate the rediscovery of that which was lost.

Many spiritual traditions link the number three to the three attributes of human nature — body, mind and spirit. For Christians, it alludes not only to the Holy Trinity, but also our call to be Priest, Prophets, and Kings. And for a Roman Catholic such as myself, Baptism, originally instituted by John – that's why they called him "The Baptist" – is the first of the three sacraments of initiation into the Church.

In the end, it's about man's quest to get closer to God. For the Hebrews in the time of Solomon, the High Priest was allowed into the Sactom Santourm once a year, on Yom Kippur, the day of atonement (or at one ment) to offer a sin offering on behalf of the people. They believed that Yahweh himself resided in that tabernacle, and for them the ark of the covenant was a sacred relic. Even today, all synagogues are directed towards the Temple Mount, where the remnants of the temple can still be seen in the Western Wall.

For Catholics, Jesus is God incarnate. By following his example of love and mercy, we hope to be reconciled with God in the hereafter. The scripture tells us that at his death on the cross, the veil of the sanctuary was torn in two, eliminating that separation between God and us that was born of original sin. The creator reuniting with his creation.

This can be seen in the way a Master Mason wears his apron. The Entered Apprentice wears his apron with the flap turned up. The spiritual is separated from the physical. The Fellowcraft wears his with the left corner tucked up. This creates two triangles. Although the Fellowcraft is attempting to imitate the divine in his own life, he falls short, for the triangle formed by the lower half of his apron does not match the triangle of the upper part of his apron. A Master Mason wears his with the flap down. The triangle of divinity coming down from heaven to unite with the square that represents man's earthly existence.

Full disclosure, I'm a firm believer that at its core, Masonry is, or rather was, a Christian organization. Despite using mostly Old Testament readings, there are breadcrumbs throughout the ritual pointing to the Christian worldview of our forebears. Operative Masons would have been Catholic, for that was the predominant religion of the day. As much as that could be a talk unto itself, I mention it because if we look at the ritual from a Christian perspective, the pieces fall into place.

Now let's look at the evidence, the various nuggets that have been left to discover. The introductory quote *"He who humbles himself will be exalted"* comes from the Gospels of both Mark and Luke and are the words of Jesus himself. In this passage, Jesus is teaching his disciples not to be like the Pharisees, who were more concerned with pomp and circumstance than with helping others. A change in understanding was needed. They had become so concerned about the proper application of the law of Moses that they missed the larger message. It's like being an excellent ritualist, able to recite long lectures flawlessly, but not living out the lessons therein contained.

If the Principal Sojourner represents John the Baptist, what is he leading to? Through the veils, which speak of the great builders, from Ham, Shem, and Jephthah, the Sons of Noah who presumably assisted in constructing the Ark, emblematic of the divine ark which was later constructed by Aholiab, Bezalel, under the direction of Moses, which resided in the first tabernacle and contained the Shekna, the Spirit of God himself. Fast forward 418 years and we encounter Jeshua, Zarubabel, and Haggi, the three worthies who helped rebuild the Temple, 70 years after the exile of the

Jewish people to Babylon. Only then do we receive the signet of Truth, which allows us into the Holy of Holies where we meet the Triune God represented by the triangular altar and the three Council officers. The great teacher, Jesus of Nazareth, of the tribe of Judah, the lion stationed in the east, stated us much when he declared "I am the way the Truth and the Light, no one comes to the Father but through me"[xxiii],

We have rebuilt our temples, not in the physical sense, but in the spiritual sense, and they have led us to the almighty, Adoni, the Lord himself, who resides in the Holy of Holies, not in the ancient city of Jerusalem, but in our hearts.

My Brothers, this concludes our journey. We have labored in the quarries, exemplified our work and been allowed to travel through the desert from the unknown to the known, from darkness to light, from confusion to truth and have found in the end he who reigns supreme, the Master of All, Jesus of Nazareth, the Son of the Ever living and True God, whose sacred name is the password by which we are recognized as his Children.

Footnotes

[i] Mt 23:12 and Lk 14:11, KJV

[ii] Is 42:16- Is 40:31, KJV

[iii] Jn 1:23, KJV

[iv] Authorized Chapter Guide, Book 4, p. 228, Grand Chapter of New York of Royal Arch Masons, 2012R Edition

[v] "Encyclopedia Of Freemasonry and it's Kindred Sciences "by ALBERT C. MACKEY M. D.

[vi] Ex 26: , Ex 26:35, Ex 27:1, Ex: 30:1 and Ex 30:6

[vii] The Biblical Tabernacle: We Catholics Would Feel at Home

[viii] Exodus Chapter 27

[ix] He 9:7

[x] Authorized Chapter Guide, Book 4, p. #, Grand Chapter of New York of Royal Arch Masons, 2012R Edition and Rv 2:17

[xi] The Symbolic Meaning of the Number Four – Master Mind Content

[xii] *Light from the Sanctuary of the Royal Arch*

[xiii] Gn 1

[xiv]15 Spiritual Meanings of 4: Symbolism Explained

[xv] Nu 2:3, Nu 2:10, Nu 2:18, Nu 2:25

[xvi] Astrological sign – Wikipedia

[xvii]How to Read an Astrology Chart: 10 Steps (with Pictures) – wikiHow

[xviii] Authorized Chapter Guide, Book 4, p. 301, Grand Chapter of New York of Royal Arch Masons, 2012R Edition

[xix] Ez 10:14

[xx] Brief History of the Analogy of the Four Evangelists to the Four Living Creatures – LXX Studies

[xxi] The Major Prophets | Bible.org

[xxii] Scribes were masters of Hebrew law, writings through diligent study – Church News

[xxiii] Jn 14:6

PART III

Supplemental Papers

The following papers submitted by members were published in newsletters or distributed in the Chapter's correspondence, but were not presented during Convocations or other events.

17

An Interpretation of the Beehive Charge

JEFFREY M. WILLIAMSON

{Summer 2023 Bulletin}

The Beehive Charge

Extend no token to the ruthless hand of ignorance. Labor at a safe distance from those who desire unearned wages and any who daub with mortar untempered. Sincerity and plain dealing distinguish the true Entered Apprentice, the arts, and sciences the engaged Fellow Craft, and unfeigned piety the honest and worthy Master Mason. Seek those qualities out, and be cautious when you do not see them in an individual who wears our apron.

Reflect further that, where silence and circumspection are not, those things that silence and circumspection are intended to preserve and guard will never be found.

Though we are all imperfect ashlars, endeavor to befriend brothers who will truly meet you on the Level and who strive to make their lives actually reflect the teachings of Freemasonry.

> Do not become overly entangled in the machinations of those who have elected not to take the wise truths of our Art seriously. Have compassion for them, and know that ones like this have always gathered near us — for even the earliest brethren wrote admonitions regarding them, both in their literature and in the very ceremonies themselves.
>
> Wish all men well, but remember the hourglass, and focus resolutely on that which you came here to do. There is no shortage of work in this Temple. Our labor is not to be concerned with the recumbent drone, but to gather what is scattered so that the hive will have honey, and the lodge greater Light.

I love this charge. It's so rich in content! I obtained it several years ago, and I like to read it from time to time just to "clear my head" and keep me centered. Let's break this charge down into pieces:

> "Extend no token to the ruthless hand of ignorance. Labor at a safe distance from those who desire unearned wages and any who daub with mortar untempered. Sincerity and plain dealing distinguish the true Entered Apprentice, the arts, and sciences the engaged Fellow Craft, and unfeigned piety the honest and worthy Master Mason. Seek those qualities out, and be cautious when you do not see them in an individual who wears our apron."

As workmen traveling along the pathway of life, we are expected to "take on" maturity, and coupled with the lessons and tools of Masonry, we are able to discern the difference between real labor and those who *labor falsely* or mistakenly or with *concealed motives*.

The first part of this charge reminds us not to get involved with those who are perverting or distorting the true intention of Freemasonry.

There are those who labor in an attempt to obtain unearned honors, using portions of Masonry to their advantage. Those who modify our teachings to suit themselves. Those who labor with untempered mortar, which will surely crumble, and not support our true Masonic edifice. We are warned to stay away from such individuals. They cause harm to our cause.

> "Reflect further that, where silence and circumspection are not, those things that silence and circumspection are intended to preserve, and guard will never be found."

There are those who dress like Masons, and disguise themselves as Masons, but they "talk the talk, but they do not walk the walk." They are like those phonies so that Jesus referred to who tear and rip up their garments and rub dirt on their faces when fasting, as if to say, "Hey, look at me … I'm fasting!" But He urged others when they fast to put on clean clothes and happy faces and let no one know you are fasting! That is how we do things in the Craft…and when giving charity, put it under a bushel basket, so it's not known to others.

Also, let us not be the first to "barge into a discussion", use prudence. Let your demeanor be such as becomes a man and Mason, thoughtful, settled, and attentive. A 33rd degree ring is adorned with three equal bands. An acquaintance of mine points to his ring and says: "Think twice before you speak once."

> "Though we are all imperfect ashlars, endeavor to befriend brothers who will truly meet you on the Level and who strive to make their lives actually reflect the teachings of Freemasonry."

It is important for every Mason to find a Lodge filled with sincere Brethren who are all on the level, striving to practice the Mystic Art.

In life, there are various circles of intimacy. We interact with acquaintances, friends, intimate friends, and spouses, and at each subsequent level, that circle becomes progressively smaller with fewer people sharing the most intimate details of our lives.

In order for a Mason to grow and prosper, he must be in a good Lodge that inculcates and encourages true labor. Sharing life with honest Brothers who care about you is essential.

If you are not in the right Lodge…find a new one that is doing the right things. Staying in a Lodge that is faulty is like being stranded in a boat without a rudder and broken sails.

> Do not become overly entangled in the machinations of those who have elected not to take the wise truths of our Art seriously. Have compassion for them and know that ones like this have always gathered near us—for even the earliest brethren wrote admonitions regarding them, both in their literature and in the very ceremonies themselves. Wish all men well, but remember the hourglass, and focus resolutely on that which you came here to do.

With ignorance of what a true Craft Lodge ought to do, some Lodges may drift into inconsequential actions that are not pertinent to our true calling as Free and Accepted Masons. We are taught that our time on this earth is limited, and therefore, we must not get caught up in petty intrigues and maneuverings. Spend your time on the important things of life.

> There is no shortage of work in this Temple. Our labor is not to be concerned with the recumbent drone, but to gather what is scattered so that the hive will have honey, and the lodge greater Light.

A drone bee is not a worker bee. It does not gather nectar or pollen. It contributes nothing for the benefit of the hive. We are admonished that we should work together as Brother Masons practicing our gentle Craft; seeking greater Light, thus enabling the Lodge and its Brethren to flourish and prosper, thereby receiving the honey of our Masonic recompense.

18

Reflections on the Holy Royal Arch

O'NEIL G.D. BRYAN

{Presented to Nassau Chapter No. 109 RAM on Monday, 13 November 2017; Emailed in December 2025 Chapter correspondence}

Why is this degree called the Holy Royal Arch?

One of the seven liberal arts and Sciences, Astronomy, is fully explored in the HRA. Time and Astronomy are inseparable, as it were. "There is a clock whose face is the sky and from which we may read forwards or backwards for thousands upon thousands of years, without the possibility of confusion, the same as we read the hours and minutes on a timepiece. This is called the Celestial Clock and refers to the Zodiac, or the pathway of the Sun through the heavens." (Light from the Sanctuary, p. 164)

Hermes Trisgemistus, or Thoth, the Egyptian God of Writing and Magic, called the Zodiac the Great Tent or Tabernaculum.

In the HRA, the Tabernacle has four veils: White, Scarlet, Blue, and Purple, and the banners bear the images of the Lion, the Bull, the Eagle, and Man, respectively. At each of these veils, there are three words, and to each division of the Zodiac, belonging to each of these stars (Aldebaran, Regulus, Fomalhaut, and Antares), there are three signs. There are also four signs, Taurus, Leo, Scorpio (the Eagle and Scorpion are synonymous), and Aquarius, which are termed the fixed signs and are appropriately assigned to the four veils. The four colors also denote the four primal elements-Air (blue), Water (purple), Fire (scarlet), and Earth (white), and are emblematical of Friendship, Union, Fervency and Zeal and Purity. These explanations you will find in our opening. (Ibid, p. 166)

What is the significance of the Grand Royal Arch Word?

We are told it is comprised of the names of deity in the languages of the Gentiles, *Jah* in the Syriac, *Bel* in the Chaldean, and *On* in the Egyptian. They represent the Triune nature of the I Am and the attributes of Deity in those languages: *Jah* = Omnipresence, *Bel* = Omnipotence, and *On* = Omniscience. Jah signifies an existence, one that is of Divine Essence, which is life-giving. In Song of Solomon 8:6, it is used to express an intense flame of fire and is therefore a fitting symbol of the omnipresence of God who is everywhere and living and active. (Lessons in Capitular Masonry, p. 54)

Bel expresses dominion. When we come to Babylonia, almighty power over all things in Heaven and Earth is attributed to Bel. He is called the "The King of all the Spirits," the "Lord of the World," "the Lord of all Countries," "The Great Lord," "He who Judges the Gods," et cetera. (Ibid, p. 60)

On was the name of a city where the sun-god was worshipped,

but On was not the name of that god. The framers of the degree had associated On with the name of Jehovah as worshipped by the Egyptians, but this is incorrect. To the better educated, or Initiates, in ancient Egypt, the many gods were mere names personifying attributes of the one True Deity. Therefore, On, the Celestial City of Egypt is the symbol of the hidden God and the hidden truth of life, which only those who had all knowledge could understand. There is only **One** who has that knowledge, and the many gods of Egypt were but manifestations of Him. His name was unknown to mortal man, and if it ever became known, man himself would become a god. For example, Isis was a mortal woman, but when she learned the true name of Ra, she became the Queen of the Gods. (Ibid, p. 63-64)

What is the "Search for the Lost Word"?

It is simply the secret doctrine of "The Ancients." Freemasonry is a philosophical attitude rather than a system of philosophy. One must be a seeker. Within its walls of tolerance, it has no place for dogma. Knowledge (or Gnosis) is not attained by institution or absorption. It may be that a few rare spirits, with subtle inherent faculties, may have at once understood and perceived many-sided **Truth** at a glance; however, most mere mortals must be content to acquire knowledge or skill by slow degrees, by practice and thought. Whatever the mystery may be, the initiate can only attain the royal secret by his own efforts. The **esoteric** admittedly implies a superior knowledge of God and man. We find and understand that the lesser mysteries taught that popular cosmogony veiled a simpler yet more subtle science; that the gods of old traditions were but the personified attributes of the Eternal and Unchanging One, the All, the Manifest Unmanifest, the Great I

Am; that man is not the result of some game of chance, but a separate entity with a definite destiny. (Ibid, p. 76-77)

Our innermost being, as men, is a manifestation of the Unknowable; a drop from the ocean of infinity, self-poised, though seemingly hedged in by time and space, in quality a god, in quantity, an atom. Man discovers himself, his God-given power, and privileges, when he ascends into the consciousness wherein power safely may be conferred upon him. He is then given the authority of **omnipotence** when he at last proves himself worthy. (Ibid, p. 80)

Furthermore, when man speaks from the height of his spiritual consciousness, God speaks through him. His word carries with it divine power; he turns upon the universal **ether** the highest possible dynamic power, one before which the powers of the world become hopelessly insignificant. The **ethers** quiver at his command and there springs into visibility the manifestation of that name of which he has called. (Ibid, p. 80)

You will find the Lost Word when you find within yourself your God-given power to create through your word. The teachers of metaphysics will necessarily raise their students to spiritual consciousness before they give them knowledge of the use of the word. It has absolutely nothing to do with the external or material, and by seeking the latter, one will surely never find the True Word. Subdue your passions and keep them in due bounds with all mankind.

Finally, Frater Bardon suggests that each religious truth is relative and the comprehension thereof depends on the maturity of the mind which seeks to unfold its mysteries. The wise one, therefore, will not impinge on any person's worldview in that regard, nor will he try to divert and distract any one man from his truth, excoriate him, to say nothing of demonizing him. However, at his core, he may truly feel sorry for fanatics and atheists without showing it outwardly, and will allow everyone to hold on to what he believes and makes him happy and content.

19

The Holy Royal Arch Degree: The Fulfillment and Climax of the Master Mason Journey

JEFFREY M. WILLIAMSON

EXPLORING SYMBOLISM, BIBLICAL FOUNDATIONS, AND DIVINE ATTRIBUTES IN FREEMASONRY

{Not previously published; emailed to members in December 2025}

Introduction

The Holy Royal Arch Degree holds a revered place within Freemasonry, often described as the climax and completion of the Master Mason degree. For centuries, Freemasons, spiritual seekers, and historians have recognized this degree as a profound spiritual journey—one that illuminates the candidate's path towards greater understanding and connection with the divine. Appreciating the Holy Royal Arch Degree requires not only an examination of its rituals and symbolism but also a thoughtful consideration of its biblical foundations and theological insights.

The Symbolic Journey: Transformative Experience of the Candidate

Central to the Holy Royal Arch Degree is the candidate's symbolic journey — a process of personal transformation, illumination, and spiritual rebirth. Unlike preceding degrees, the Royal Arch does not merely build upon the teachings of the Master Mason Degree, but rather brings them to their fulfillment. Candidates are invited to embark on a quest that transcends mere allegory, encouraging an inward reflection on the mysteries of faith, perseverance, and ultimate truth.

This journey is marked by trials and revelations, mirroring the spiritual quest for enlightenment. The candidate's passage through the degree is not only a reenactment of ancient stories but also a metaphor for the search for hidden wisdom and the restoration of that which was lost. In the Royal Arch, the seeker finds not just completion, but the true meaning behind the foundations laid in previous degrees.

Biblical Foundations: Moses, the Burning Bush, and the Divine Name

The Holy Royal Arch Degree draws extensively from biblical symbolism, most notably the account of Moses and the burning bush described in the Book of Exodus. When Moses encounters God in the form of a burning bush, he asks for the divine name. God responds, "I AM THAT I AM," a statement rich in theological significance and mystery. This revelation is central to the Royal Arch, representing the unveiling of sacred knowledge and the direct encounter with the divine presence.

This biblical narrative serves as the cornerstone of the degree's teachings. The burning bush is a symbol of the enduring and unconsumed spirit, while the revelation of the divine name points to the ineffable nature of God—a reality that cannot be fully grasped or articulated by human understanding. The degree encourages candidates to approach this mystery with reverence, humility, and a willingness to seek deeper truths.

Understanding the Attributes of God: Omnipresence, Omniscience, and Omnipotence

Within the Holy Royal Arch Degree, candidates are invited to contemplate the attributes of God as revealed through scripture and Masonic tradition. The divine name "I AM THAT I AM" encapsulates the qualities of God: His omnipresence (present everywhere), omniscience (all-knowing), and omnipotence (all-powerful). These attributes are not mere abstractions; they are explored through the rituals and teachings of the degree as essential aspects of spiritual reality.

Through allegory and symbolism, the degree guides candidates to recognize that God is ever-present in the world and in the lives of those who seek Him. It affirms that divine wisdom is accessible to the sincere and diligent, and that ultimate power rests not in earthly authority, but in the transcendent source of all being. The contemplation of these attributes encourages a deeper sense of awe, responsibility, and spiritual purpose.

The Allegory of the Three Most Excellent Masters: From

Babylon to Jerusalem

One of the defining allegories of the Holy Royal Arch Degree is the journey of three Most Excellent Masters who travel from Babylon to Jerusalem to rebuild the Temple of God. This tale is rich in symbolism, reflecting themes of exile, perseverance, and spiritual restoration. The journey from Babylon—a place of captivity and separation—towards Jerusalem, the holy city, mirrors the candidate's own passage from ignorance to enlightenment.

The Masters face numerous struggles: the challenges of the journey, the obstacles in rebuilding, and the uncertainties of the quest. Yet, their perseverance is ultimately rewarded by the discovery of the lost treasures and, most significantly, the Great and Sacred Name of God. This narrative teaches that spiritual progress is achieved not through ease, but through steadfast faith, resilience, and the willingness to seek that which is hidden.

Discovery of the Sacred Name: Significance and Meaning

The climax of the Royal Arch narrative is the discovery of the Sacred Name—a symbol of the ultimate truth and divine presence. This name, revealed to Moses and sought by generations, represents the fulfillment of the Master Mason degree and the restoration of lost wisdom. For the candidate, this moment is not simply the acquisition of knowledge, but a transformative experience that brings together the lessons of perseverance, faith, and spiritual vision.

The significance of the Sacred Name in Freemasonry is manifold. It serves as a reminder of the divine source from which all wisdom flows, and of the sacred duty to honor that source through righteous living and sincere seeking. The revelation of the Name is a call to humility and reverence, affirming that the deepest mysteries of existence are accessible to those who approach with pure intent and unwavering dedication.

Conclusion: The Importance of the Holy Royal Arch Degree in Freemasonry

The Holy Royal Arch Degree stands as the fulfillment and climax of the Master Mason journey, offering a profound synthesis of symbolism, biblical foundation, and spiritual insight. By guiding candidates through a transformative allegorical journey, rooted in the story of Moses and the attributes of God, the degree fosters a deeper appreciation for the mysteries of faith and the pursuit of truth. For Freemasons, spiritual seekers, and historians, the Royal Arch remains a testament to the enduring power of allegory, the transformative potential of ritual, and the eternal quest for divine wisdom.

20

Rabboni, The Most Excellent Master

GREGORY D. MACLEOD

{Published in December 2025 Chapter correspondence.}

Background – In progressing through the degrees of the Holy Royal Arch there are may lessons which can be extracted. The deeply allegorical ritual expands upon the lessons of the first three degrees. This paper focus on the Most Excellent Master degree.

One of the seminal events in the Most Excellent Master Degree is the completion of the Temple. All of our labors have been completed. The craftsmen can finally remove their aprons and reflect on a job well done. What deeper lessons is this degree trying to teach? What does the temple represent, and did it even exist historically or is it only allegorical in nature?

First some history; every good Mason ought to know that it took a little more then seven years to complete the construction of the temple.[i] Most of our knowledge of the temple comes from Biblical sources, namely the 1 and 2 Kings and 1 and 2 Chronicles. Written down circa 550 BCE and 438 BCE respectively [ii], these books cover the time from 1003 BCE to 586 BCE[iii], including the reign of King Solomon, which began in 967 BCE[iv] and lasted for 40 years[v] (to 927 BCE). It should be noted that, although the Temple was named after King Solomon, his father David, designed it, and Hiram helped oversee its construction, thus all Solomon did was finance the project. Such it is today, as many of the great buildings are named not for the laborers who built it, nor the architects who designed it, but for the family that put up the money. Thus Solomon gets the credit and the Temple is attributed to his name.

Despite the mention of the project in detail in two biblical books, there is a lack of secondary sources to prove that the temple ever existed. Given the current political climate in the area, excavating under the temple mount will not happen any time soon.[vi] Of course, legend indicates that the Poor Knights of Christ and the Temple of Solomon, also known at the Knights Templar[vii], discovered "something" under the Temple Mount, which lead to their rapid assent to fame and fortune, and may have even played a role in their snuffing out in 1307 on Friday October 13, a day that even today is associated with ill fortune.[viii] But what they may have found, be it riches or the Ark of the Covenant itself, we will never know.

The lack of evidence for this first Temple notwithstanding, we do know without a doubt that there was a second temple, for the Western or Wailing Wall, still exists and is a sacred place for modern day Jews to congregate and offer up their prayers and petitions to the everlasting and True God. History tells us this second temple was expanded by King Herod about the time of Christ. The historian Flavius Josepus, a Roman Jewish scribe and historian, wrote of the how the second temple was expanded by Herod then subsequently was razed in 70 AD after the siege of Jerusalem.[ix],[x]

Further, given that the exile period in Babylon lasted roughly 70 years, from 597 BCE to 539[xi], it is not inconceivable that a twenty-year-old who was taken into exile could have returned to the ruins of Jerusalem at the age of ninety and even live to see the temple partially, if not fully restored. The Bible tells us that the elders wept when they saw the foundation of the new temple being laid (Ez 3:12); further strengthening the postulation that King Solomon's Temple did, in fact, exist prior to the Babylonian Exile. Although the scripture describes a mixture of tears of sorrow and shouts of joy, the weeping of the elders is interpreted by scripture scholars as an indication that the second temple built by Zerubbabel and his associates did not match the grandeur of Solomon's original.[xii]

Now, it is conceivable that the original edifice was expanded over the years by subsequent Kings, given that this first temple stood for over 500 years. But if that did occur, it was not seen fit to record in the Biblical sources. Joash repaired and rebuilt the temple "according to original design and reinforced it." (2 Chr 24:13) at some point during his reign (818 BCE to 778 BCE). King Hezekiah (665 BCE to 636 BCE) repaired the temple, expanded the courtyard, built a tunnel to bring in water, and strengthened the walls to better protect the edifice, but an extensive remodeling was, at least according to Biblical sources, not done.[xiii] Finally, Josiah oversaw another extensive repair in 561 BCE. So it seems that every hundred years or so, the temple was repaired, presumably to its former glory, leading us to surmise that the Temple David designed and Solomon built was relatively unchanged from its erection in 967 BCE until its destruction in 424 BCE[xiv].

Thus, its original dimensions, as set forth in 1 Chronicles and 1 Kings, were 60 cubits long by 20 cubits wide by 30 cubits high, with a cubit being the length of one's arm from the elbow to the fingertips, generally accepted to be equivalent to 18 inches. Therefore, the temple would have been 90 ft long by 30 ft wide and 45 ft tall, and given its location on top of Mount Moriah, it would have been visible from miles away. It should be noted that Solomon's Palace, although larger in footprint, was no taller. Perhaps it was the limitations of architecture at the time, or more probably, they did not want to build anything that would eclipse the Temple, similar to how, for almost a century, buildings in Philadelphia were limited to be no taller than 548 ft, lest they eclipse the Statue of William Penn atop City Hall.[xv]

As with most of the degrees, particularly those of the York Rite, there are Christian undercurrents throughout. Psalm XXIV, verses 5 through 10 is recited during the perambulations, which discusses the King of Glory; a reference to the coming Messiah who, for Christians, is Christ Jesus of Nazareth.

Further, the name of the cover grip is *Rabboni*, a term which is used only twice in the entire Bible, both in the New Testament; the Gospels of Mark (10:51) and John (Jn 20:16) respectively. In Mark, Jesus was approached by a blind man named Bartimaeus who wanted his site restored, and was healed by his faith in the Lord.

> So Jesus answered and said to him [Bartimaeus], "What do you want Me to do for you?" The blind man said to Him, "Rabboni, that I may

> receive my sight."Then Jesus said to him, "Go your way; your faith has made you well." And immediately he received his sight and followed Jesus on the road. – Mk 10:51-52 (NKJV)

In John, Rabboni are the first words said by Mary Magdalene when she recognizes the Resurrected Jesus at the tomb on Easter morning, a critical moment in the development of what became Christianity.

> But Mary stood outside by the tomb weeping, and as she wept she stooped down and looked into the tomb. And she saw two angels in white sitting, one at the head and the other at the feet, where the body of Jesus had lain. Then they said to her, "Woman, why are you weeping?" She said to them, "Because they have taken away my Lord, and I do not know where they have laid Him." Now when she had said this, she turned around and saw Jesus standing there, and did not know that it was Jesus. Jesus said to her, "Woman, why are you weeping? Whom are you seeking?" She, supposing Him to be the gardener, said to Him, "Sir, if You have carried Him away, tell me where You have laid Him, and I will take Him away." Jesus said to her, "Mary!" She turned and said to Him, "Rabboni!" (which is to say, Teacher). Jesus said to her, "Do not cling to Me, for I have not yet ascended to My Father; but go to My brethren and say to them, 'I am ascending to My Father and your Father, and to My God and your God.'" Mary Magdalene came and told the disciples that she had seen the Lord, and that He had spoken these things to her. – Jn 20:11-18 (NKJV)

Now the term *Rabbi or Rabboni*, which literally means *Master* in Hebrew, and roughly translated means "Teacher" or "Great Teacher" respectively. [xvi] The term originated sometime in the first century CE, thus Solomon would never have been refereed to as, or refereed to someone else as *Rabboni*.[xvii] It should also be noted that historically, the Holy Royal Arch degrees and the Most Excellent Master degree which precedes it, were originally conferred only on Actual Masters of Lodges, thus a term meaning "*My Master*" or "*My Teacher*" is wholly appropriate from a Masonic perspective, even if the use of the term is not fully historically accurate but more allegorical in nature. As Royal Arch Masons we are called to teach our brethren to the best of our ability. In some ways the completion of the temple can be seen as a graduation of sorts. As Most Excellent Masters we have wrought in the quarries and exemplified our work. We not only are well versed in right angles, horizontals, and perpendiculars, we have been taught the secrets of how to use the square and compasses to construct curves and arches, moving beyond the simple to more complex geometries.

The ritual of the Most Excellent Master indicates Solomon greets the Master Builder with these words (*Raboni*). We know that Masonically, Hiram Abiff was the Master Builder, as the chief artificer of the temple[xviii], and the Hiramic Legend portrayed in the Master Mason degree indicates that he was slain prior to its completion.[xix] So who could Solomon be greeting? Neither biblical, apocryphal or Masonic sources indicate any other candidates. Further, if Solomon, whose Wisdom was well established (1 Kgs 4:29-34), had referred someone else as a Teacher, certainly this would have been recorded in Biblical sources. So who is this mysterious person?

A careful examination of the ritual shows the WE who have received this degree are the Master Builders, for King Solomon and King Hiram each takes the candidate by the hand and "*receive and acknowledge [him] as a most excellent master*". It is meant to teach us that we have ascended, through our service, to a lofty position.

Recall also the Mark Master Obligation. Among the furthermores, we are called to dispense *True Masonic Light* – what is true masonic light? First, given the placement of the Most Excellent Degree immediately after the Past Master Degree, the candidate is presumed to exemplify the Wisdom of King Solomon, having served as Master of his Lodge "virtually" if not in reality. Thus we who have received the Most Excellent Master Degree have by virtue of our Masonic labors up to this point, have knowledge and experience that we can share with others.

But there is still more light to be dispensed. Go back to the healing of the blind man. He who formerly was in darkness now can see. Are we not called to do the same? What is the role of the Principal Sojourner in the Royal Arch? Leading the blind, and making crooked paths straight, a reference to John the Baptist. Even the dedication ode is sung to the tune of "*Oh Come All Ye Faithful*", which sings about people being flocking to Bethlehem to adore the Infant Jesus. We cannot fully appreciate the tapestry that is the Royal Arch System without viewing it through a Christian lense.

Why did they wait a year between the completion and the dedication? The Temple was completed in eight months (1 Kgs 6:38) but not dedicated until the seventh month of the following year

(1 Kgs 8:2) during the Jewish holiday of Sukkot, also known as the Feast of Tabernacles or the Feast of Booths. The origins of this Harvest feast go back to the time of Moses (Lv 23:22-43), and is so termed because the Jews are called upon to live in temporary shelters for seven days, representing the temporary shelter they lived in upon their exodus from Egypt and the original tabernacle built by Moses which was a portable tent used to house the Ark of the Covenant until such time as a permanent resting place

could be established. This resting place was, of course, the Sanctum Sanctorum of King Solomon's Temple!

Thus it would be symbolic to use the feast of Sukkot as the appropriate time to dedicate the Temple. Some have postulated that the delay of almost a full year was simply to give proper time to plan such a large celebration. I put forth an alternate explanation. We know from the third degree that the temple was progressing on schedule until the Murder of Grand Master Hiram Abiff. We know from the Mark Master that a certain keystone, wrought by Hiram Abiff, was inadvertently thrown in the rubbish and for a brief period of time, lost. It is not hard to imagine the disruption that Hiram's passing would have caused among the workmen, King Solomon, and Hiram, King of Tyre.

Had the original schedule not been upended, the Temple would have been completed in the seventh month rather than stretching into the eighth. Solomon would probably have already sent out invitations to the dedication ceremony well in advance, thus dignitaries would have been planning their arrival, if not already in transit. One could see Solomon in his wisdom using what was supposed to have been a joyous dedication and re-purposing it as a memorial service for his dearly departed friend, intentionally delaying the dedication ceremony until the following year, because it would be an offense to his memory to dedicate the temple before the requisite thirty days of mourning were over. This would also explain the re-interment of Hiram's body as close to the Temple Mount as Jewish law would allow.

Solomon, in his dedication prayer, asks, "*Will God in very deed dwell with men on the Earth?*" For Christians, the answer to that question is an emphatic yes. Although Psalm 24 asks, "Who is this King of Glory?" The answer can be found in the password *Rab-*

boni. Men who were heretofore blind finally "see. They encounter Jesus in a real and deeply personal way, as did Mary Magdalene at his tomb, when she was the first to encounter the Resurrected Jesus.

What are the deeper lessons? No matter how great we are, no matter how much we accomplish, we have a finite time here on earth and will one day pass on. Even King Solomon's temple was not spared the ravages of barbarous force. The second temple, rebuilt on the ruins of the first, was also destroyed.

Even Jesus descended to the dead before being raised to heaven. No one is immune. However as the first degree teaches us, if we have faith, if we live by the precepts found in the volume of scared law, then our soul will find its way to that perfect temple, that house not made with hands, eternal in the heavens and when our feet come to the end of their toilsome journey and the working tools fall forever from our grasp, may it be our portion to hear from him who sitteth as the Judge Supreme, "*Well done, good and faithful servant, enter into the joy of thy Lord.*"

Footnotes

[i] Standard Work, Grand Lodge of the State of New York

[ii] When Was Each Book of the Bible Written? | Bible Gateway News & Knowledge

[iii] Bible Timeline

[iv] King Solomon

[v] 2 Chronicles 9:30

[vi] Jerusalem's Temples: The Archaeological Evidence | ArmstrongInstitute.org

[vii] Templar | History, Battles, Symbols, & Legacy | Britannica

[viii] Arrest order of Templars who were in France – Rota dos Templários

[ix] Flavius Josephus | Jewish Priest, Scholar, Historian of 1st Century Judea | Britannica

[x] Second Temple – Wikipedia

[xi] Babylonian Exile – Bible Odyssey

[xii] Topical Bible: Joy and Weeping at the Temple Foundation

[xiii] Hezekiah – Wikipedia

[xiv] The Destruction of the First Holy Temple – Chabad.org

[xv] Philadelphia City Hall – Wikipedia

[xvi] Was Jesus a Rabbi? – Jew in the City

[xvii] Rabboni – BiblePortal Wikipedia

[xviii] Standard Work, Grand Lodge of the State of New York

[xix] Freemasonry and King Solomon's Temple | Freemasonry

21

The Hermetic Order of the Golden Dawn

BRETT LAIRD FRANCIS DOYLE

{Presented at one or more Chapters by the author, submitted on 6 February 2026, and to be sent out in the TSW newsletter before Grand Convocation in March. Brett Doyle is Past High Priest of Army Chapter No.393, San Antonio Chapter No.381, and Cooper Chapter No.101, a member of Thomas Smith Webb Chapter of Research No.1798, the Texas Lodge of Research, and an Active Member of the American Lodge of Research.}

The Hermetic Order of the Golden Dawn is a non-masonic organization which formed in the 19th century and is often associated with Freemasonry. The Order was developed in the late 19th century with the discovery of the Cipher Manuscripts.

The Cipher Manuscripts were passed between several masonic scholars until William Wynn Westcott was able to decode them in 1887. Westcott shared the Cipher Manuscripts with fellow Freemason Samuel Liddell MacGregor Mathers for a second opinion. Mathers in turn shared the findings with another Freemason, William Robert Woodman. Mathers and Westcott are credited with developing the decoding of the Cipher Manuscripts into a usable format. Within the Cipher Manuscripts, Westcott found the name and address of Anna Sprengel, a woman living in Germany, which Westcott made contact with Sprengel, who claimed to be in contact with the Secret Chiefs, beings who are responsible for overseeing all matters pertaining to esoteric organizations.[1]

Westcott asked Sprengel for permission to form a new temple in London, which Sprengel gave permission for and made Westcott, Mathers and Woodman members of the Order in 1887. These three leveraged their Masonic and Rosicrucian backgrounds to create a coed, non-Masonic esoteric society focused on Hermeticism, Qabalah, and ritual magic, distinct from the SRIA's Christian and male-only requirements. It should be noted that there is some speculation that the Secret Chiefs, although often described as beings, are also believed to have books and materials containing esoteric knowledge.[2]

Although some of the founders of the Order of the Golden Dawn were Freemasons, the Societas Rosicruciana in Anglia (S.R.I.A.) is a recognized fraternal order founded in England in 1867, dedicated to esoteric and mystical studies, particularly Rosicrucianism. It restricts membership to Master Masons who are also Christians, focusing on spiritual and philosophical exploration through rituals and teachings inspired by Rosicrucian traditions. The Order of the Golden Dawn had a similar system of three orders with three degrees that were similar to the following primary S.R.I.A. degrees:

1. Zelator
2. Theoricus
3. Practicus

The Golden Dawn's First Order degrees, in particular, align closely with the SRIA's initial grades in name and thematic focus, though their rituals and teachings differ due to the Golden Dawn's emphasis on practical magic and Hermetic Qabalah.

The first order, sometimes referred to as the Outer Order, consists of six grades. The second order, which at one point was the ruling order of the Order of the Golden Dawn, has three grades. The final order has two grades.[3]

Whilst on the other hand, the Order of the Golden Dawn had no gender requirements or masonic affiliation requirements. Women were allowed into the Order on an equal standing with men. One of the members who joined during the Golden age of the Order in the mid-1890's was Florence Farr, a popular actress at the time. She would become closely associated with Mathers until the two had a falling out over Aleister Crowley in the early 1900's.[4]

A. E. Waite joined the Hermetic Order of the Golden Dawn in 1891, where he encountered Aleister Crowley, and later left in 1914 due to internal strife. In 1896 or 1897, Westcott broke ties with the Order leaving Mathers in charge. It is unclear why Westcott left the order. It has been said that Westcott left documents concerning the Order in a hansom cab, which was a horse-drawn carriage. When his employer was informed, he was a coroner at the time, he was given the choice to leave the Order or resign from his job. However, Westcott left the organization, it was the beginning of change in the order. By the early 1900's, several temples of the Order had decided to declare their independence, generally unhappy with Mather's leadership. Some famous Freemasons and non-masons who were associated with the order were Aleister Crowley, Arthur Conan Doyle and A.E. Waite.[5]

To our utter surprise back in 1983, my best friend, Edward Charles Volkert III, made a pen and ink portrait that was later made into a lithograph and printed on the 30th of April 1984 (see after footnotes). If one looks closely, the two points to notice inside the lithograph are images of the back of a Thoth Tarot card deck and Aleister Crowley. In modern lithography, this black and white image is made from a polymer coating applied to a flexible plastic or metal plate to produce initially a proof followed by more high quality prints.[6] The original plastic plate & proof is in the Smithsonian Museum, Washington, DC, in the "Edward Charles Volkert The First" collection.[7]

Footnotes

[1] "The Golden Dawn", by Israel Regardie; 1937.

[2] Ibid.

[3] Ibid.

[4] https://study.com/academy/lesson/hermetic-order-golden-dawn-origin-role-beliefs.html

[5] https://freemasonry.bcy.ca/aqc/waite/waite.html

[6] https://www.metmuseum.org/about-the-met/collection-areas/drawings-and-prints/materials-and-techniques/printmaking/lithograph

[7] https://www.aaa.si.edu/collections/edward-c-volkert-papers-6922

About the Chapter

The Thomas Smith Webb Chapter of Research was warranted on August 2, 2002, by the Grand Chapter, State of New York, Royal Arch Masons. It is the first such chapter so authorized. The purpose of the Chapter is to encourage Royal Arch Masonic Research and study by its members and others, to present findings and conclusions to the Chapter for discussion and interchange, and to promote the discussion and debate of topics pertinent to Royal Arch Masonry.

Membership is by affiliation only. The Chapter does not confer degrees. All Royal Arch Masons who are members, in good standing, of a Chapter in jurisdictions recognized by The Grand Chapter State of New York, Royal Arch Masons are eligible for membership. There are three classes of membership: Active Membership is open to any Royal Arch Mason who is a member in good standing of a Chapter under the jurisdiction of the Grand Chapter State of New York; Corresponding Membership is open to any Royal Arch Mason, or member of a Concordant Body recognized by The Grand Chapter State of New York, Royal Arch Masons; Fellowship is an honor conferred upon a Royal Arch Mason for outstanding achievement in Masonic research and publication. Individual Chapters, Grand Chapters, and recognized

Concordant bodies may petition for Corresponding Membership. Other Masonic Research bodies are also eligible for membership, including libraries. The right to ballot and to hold office is vested in Active Members only.

FOR MORE INFORMATION AND A PETITION TO AFFILIATE, GO TO TSW.NYRAM.ORG

OFFICERS (2025-2026)

E∴ Ken JP Stuczynski – High Priest
E∴ Chris Fox – King
V∴E∴ Michael Chaplin – Scribe
E∴ Anthony Giannattasio – Treasurer
Comp. Noel Ventegeat – Secretary
R∴E∴ Walter Leong – Chaplain
R∴E∴ Keith Dash – Captain of the Host
V∴E∴ Victor Escorbares – Principal Sojourner
E∴ O'Neil Bryan – Royal Arch Captain
E∴ Asly Raymond – Master of the 3rd Veil
Comp. Victor Marshall – Master of the 2nd Veil
Comp. Gregory Macleod – Master of the 1st Veil
R∴E∴ Rich Larson – Sentinel

FELLOWS

R∴E∴ Grant Held
R∴E∴ Oscar Alleyne
M∴E∴ Piers Vaughan
M∴E∴ Jeffrey M. Williamson

R.·.E.·. Stephen A. Rubinstein – Founder & Honorary High Priest

R.·.E.·. John Mauk Hilliard – 2002

R.·.E.·. John Mauk Hilliard – 2003

M.·.E.·. Edmund D. Harrison – 2004

R.·.E.·. William Zufall – 2005

R.·.E.·. Mark L. Adler – 2006-2007

R.·.E.·. Jeffrey M. Williamson – 2008

R.·.E.·. Kenneth Fischer – 2009

V.·.E.·. James Stoll – 2010

R.·.E.·. Leon B. Weinstein – 2011

R.·.E.·. Grant Held – 2022

M.·.E.·. Jeffrey M. Williamson – 2023

R.·.E.·. James Gregg – 2024

By-Laws

THE THOMAS S. WEBB CHAPTER NO.1798
FOR ROYAL ARCH RESEARCH (THE WEBB CHAPTER)
BY-LAWS

ARTICLE I. – NAME

The Chapter shall be known and distinguished as THE THOMAS SMITH WEBB CHAPTER No. 1798 OF ROYAL ARCH RESEARCH (THE WEBB CHAPTER), hereinafter referred to as the Chapter, under the jurisdiction of the Grand Chapter of the State of New York, Royal Arch Masons, hereinafter referred to as the Grand Chapter.

ARTICLE II. – PURPOSES

The purpose of the Chapter is to encourage Royal Arch Masonic research and study by its members and others; to present findings and conclusions to the Chapter for discussion and interchange of judgment; to sponsor discussion and debate topics pertaining to Royal Arch Masonry and to publish Transactions at convenient intervals, containing such portions of the addresses, discussions and debates as may be desirable to print. The Chapter is not authorized nor permitted to confer degrees, although exemplification of degrees for research purposes may be permitted.

ARTICLE III. – CONVOCATIONS

SECTION 1: The Annual Convocation of the Chapter shall be held before, after, or during events in the Grand Convocation schedule. The time and location shall be as ordered by the High Priest, and convenient to the location of Grand Chapter's proceedings.

SECTION 2: Other convocations shall be special convocations, at such time and place as ordered by the High Priest.

SECTION 3: Special Convocations may be called by the High Priest at Masonic meeting places within or without the State of New York, subject to and in accordance with any required dispensation to be obtained from the Grand Chapter of another jurisdiction.

SECTION 4: Nine Members, including the High Priest or one of the Council Officers, of the Chapter, shall constitute a quorum for the transaction of business at a Stated Convocation of the Chapter.

SECTION 4.1: At any Special Convocation, nine Companions must be present, including the High Priest or one of the Council Officers of the Chapter.

ARTICLE IV. – OFFICERS

SECTION 1: A High Priest, King, Scribe, Treasurer, and Secretary shall be elected annually. One of three Trustees shall be elected annually for a three-year term, except that in the first year, three Trustees shall be elected, the terms of whose offices shall be, respectively, one year, two years, and three years.

SECTION 2: The High Priest shall appoint a Captain of the Host, a Principal Sojourner, a Royal Arch Captain. Masters of the First, Second, and Third Veils, and a Sentinel, and one or more Chaplains.

SECTION 3: The High Priest shall appoint and designate such committees as may be necessary or desirable for the conduct of the business of the Chapter.

SECTION 4: Elected officers and trustees must be active members of the Chapter. Appointed officers must be active members of the Chapter.

SECTION 5: The High Priest of the Chapter must have previously been elected, installed, and served as High Priest in another Chapter under the jurisdiction of the Grand Chapter.

ARTICLE V. – OFFICER DUTIES

SECTION 1: The Treasurer shall receive from the Secretary all money paid into the Chapter and shall give his receipt thereof, keep a just and regular account thereof, and deposit the same in such bank, trust company, or savings institution as the Chapter may designate. All money shall be deposited in the name of the Chapter and no withdrawal shall be made except by check signed by the Treasurer or the Secretary upon authorization by the Chapter.

SECTION 1.1: The Treasurer shall arrange for or provide copies of financial statements to the Secretary in a timely manner, and not more than two weeks after statements are posted.

SECTION 2: The Secretary shall record the proceedings of the Chapter under the direction of the High Priest. He shall receive all money paid into the Chapter and pay the same to the Treasurer, taking his receipt therefore, and shall accurately keep such books and records, and perform such duties, as prescribed by the Grand Chapter. The Secretary may directly deposit monies received, with copies of checks and deposit tickets being forwarded to the Treasurer.

SECTION 3: The Trustees shall be elected and their duties performed in accordance with the New York Benevolent Orders Law, including the requirement of their residency in New York State.

ARTICLE VI. – MEMBERSHIP

SECTION 1: There shall be two classes of Members in the Chapter: Members and Fellows, as well as Subscribers, who shall not be considered Members.

SECTION 2: Membership shall be acquired by affiliation only and application is open to Royal Arch Masons in good standing of Chapters under the jurisdiction of the Grand Chapter and in jurisdictions recognized by Grand Chapter. Petitions from applicants shall be received and acted upon in accordance with the Constitution of Grand Chapter, except that such petitions may be acted upon during special as well as stated communications.

SECTION 3: Subscribers may be any person or entity, such as a library or Masonic Lodge or body, and shall have access to all publications, digitally at no cost or the same price as for Members if in any physical format.

SECTION 3.1: Subscribers must be elected by a majority "show of hands" at any Stated Convocation, and do not require prior notice.

SECTION 4: Fellowship is an honor to be conferred upon Royal Arch Masons for outstanding achievement in Masonic research and publication. It may be conferred upon any active member in good standing, by the unanimous ballot of the Active Members of the Chapter at any Convocation thereof, after proposal in open Chapter and prior notice to the Membership.

SECTION 5: The right to vote ballot and hold office in the Chapter shall be limited to Members; Members who are elected to Fellowship shall continue to have all the rights, privileges, and benefits of Members to vote, ballot and hold office in the Chapter.

SECTION 6.1: Every Member shall advise the Secretary of their current mailing address and contact information.

SECTION 6: Every Member shall receive the meeting notices of the Chapter and the published Transactions or proceedings thereof, if any.

SECTION 7: Subscribers who are current in the payment of dues shall receive all publications of the Chapter, including Notices. Subscribership by an organization shall not, by virtue thereof, confer the right to attend meetings upon any individual.

ARTICLE VII. – FEES AND DUES

SECTION 1: Petitioners for Membership shall pay an affiliation fee of ten ($10) dollars, even if previously a Subscriber.

SECTION 2: Annual dues are payable in advance on or before the beginning of each calendar year. Annual dues for Members shall be twenty ($20) dollars; annual dues for Subscribers (Corresponding Members) shall be twenty ($20) dollars. Dues are not prorated. However, members elected in the last three months of the calendar year shall not be responsible for that year's dues.

SECTION 3: Fellows shall be exempt from the payment of any and all dues and fees.

SECTION 4: Subscribers who are elected to Membership shall pay the dues of a Member in the year elected, and if such Member shall have already paid the dues of a Subscriber, he shall pay an additional sum as dues in the year elected to Membership in an amount equal to the difference in dues between that for Subscribers and Members.

SECTION 5: Subscribers whose dues shall remain unpaid as of December 31st in any year shall be dropped from Subscription. Members one year in arrears of dues (365 elapsed days) may be unaffiliated by a majority vote of the Chapter, taken by a show of hands at any Convocation, provided such Member shall have been duly summoned at least thirty (30) days prior thereto to pay said arrears of dues and the same shall remain unpaid. Publications, if any, will be withheld from any Member or subscriber or Subscriber who is not current in their dues.

ARTICLE VIII. – PROCEEDINGS

SECTION 1: The Chapter. at convenient intervals. may publish proceedings or transactions containing such portions of the addresses and discussions presented in Chapter or submitted thereto, as may be deemed appropriate. It may also publish, reproduce, print or reprint original books of Masonic merit, Masonic documents of historical significance, and rare Masonic publications of all kinds.

SECTION 2: A Publications Committee appointed by the High Priest shall be in charge of the compilation, manufacture, and distribution of all publications of the Chapter.

SECTION 2.1: The Chapter, at its discretion, may make available publications outside of Membership and Subscribers. Printed content will be sold at prices set by the Excellent High Priest to cover the costs of printing, postage, and transaction fees.

ARTICLE IX. – AMENDMENTS

A proposition to amend or annul any or all of these by-laws, or to substitute others in their stead, shall be made in writing, subscribed by three Active Members, read before the Chapter without discussion, and shall then lie over until the next Stated Convocation, to which the Chapter shall be summoned for a vote. The full text of the proposition shall be published, together with the existing provisions, if any, in the Chapter meeting notice for such summoned Convocation. The assent of 2/3 of the Active Members present shall adopt such proposition. Any amendment to the proposition may be made before the vote at such summoned Convocation without further notice.

A revision to the by-laws is approved by the Standing Committee on By-Laws of the Grand Chapter, State of New York, Royal Arch Masons in accordance with Section 325 of the Grand Chapter Constitution. No revision shall take effect until the conditions set forth in Section 325 shall be met.

{Modified and Approved 13 October 2023 at a Convocation in Buffalo, NY}

About the Publisher

cyphrGlyffe is the esoteric imprint of Amorphous Publishing Guild, owned and operated by Bro. Ken JP Stuczynski, author of "Webmastering the Craft" (2020) and "Masonic Research Lodges, Bodies, and Societies" (2024). All titles are available worldwide. For more information, visit **www.Amorphous.Press/cyphrglyffe/**.

www.ingramcontent.com/pod-product-compliance
Ingram Content Group UK Ltd.
Pitfield, Milton Keynes, MK11 3LW, UK
UKHW020143250726
13967UKWH00002B/837

9 781949 818215